Early Portland:
STUMP-TOWN TRIUMPHANT

1831 Rival Townsites On the Willamette **1854**

By Eugene E. Snyder

Binford & Mort
Publishing

2536 S.E. Eleventh • Portland, Oregon 97202

Early Portland: STUMP-TOWN TRIUMPHANT

Copyright © 1970 by Binfords & Mort, Publishers

Manufactured in the United States of America

Library of Congress Catalog Card Number: 83-73372
ISBN: 0-8323-0218-X (hardcover); 0-8323-0295-3 (softcover)
First Edition 1970
Second Edition 1984

CONTENTS

A *List of the Early Townsites* v

To the Reader vii

1. The Setting 1
2. Two Who Were Too Soon............................... 3
3. Fort Vancouver: Not a Contender..................... 12
4. Oregon City's Early Advantages...................... 18
5. Rival Townsites at the Falls........................ 27
6. The Flourishing Village of Portland................. 30
7. Portland's Pettygrove Period....................... 35
8. Gold Hits the Townsites............................ 47
9. An Energetic Rival at Milwaukie.................... 55
10. The Portland Trio.................................. 64
11. A New Weapon: The Printing Press.................. 72
12. The First Steamships 81
13. Milwaukie's Glory: The "Lot Whitcomb" 92
14. Navigational Difficulties 107
15. Milwaukie: Decline and Fall......................113
16. Rival Proprietors Downstream.....................126
17. Threats of Roads and Railroads...................142
18. The Great Plank Road 150
19. The Battle for the Steamship Line................155
20. A New Steamship Brings Victory 168
    Epilogue 173
    Notes 177
    Index 179

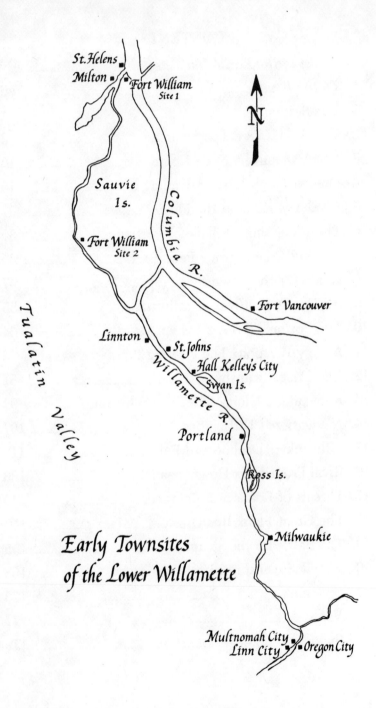

St. Helens
Milton
Fort William
Site 1

N

Columbia R.

Sauvie
Is.

Fort William
Site 2

Fort Vancouver

Tualatin Valley

Linnton

St. Johns

Hall Kelley's City

Swan Is.

Willamette R.

Portland

Ross Is.

Milwaukie

Early Townsites
of the Lower Willamette

Multnomah City
Linn City
Oregon City

A LIST OF THE EARLY TOWNSITES
ALONG THE LOWER WILLAMETTE RIVER

Hall Kelley's City: Envisioned in a pamphlet published by Hall J. Kelley at Boston in 1831. It would have been where north Portland is today. It existed only on paper.

Fort William: Established by Nathaniel Wyeth on Sauvie Island in 1834. Abandoned in 1836.

Oregon City: Laid out as a townsite and named by Dr. John McLoughlin in 1842. A Hudson's Bay Co. trading post had been there since 1829.

Linn City: Laid out in 1842 by Robert Moore on his claim of 1841. Now part of West Linn.

Multnomah City: Laid out by Hugh Burns on a claim he established about 1843. Now part of West Linn.

Portland: Development was begun by Lovejoy and Pettygrove in 1844. The site had first been claimed by Overton in 1843.

Linnton: Development was begun in 1845 by Peter Burnett and Morton McCarver, on their claim of 1844. Now part of Portland.

Milwaukie: Established in 1848 by Lot Whitcomb on a land claim he acquired that year. He was joined by Kellogg, Luelling, and Torrence.

St. Helens: An undeveloped claim here was acquired in 1847 by Henry M. Knighton. Active development began in 1850. William Tappan worked with Knighton.

Milton: The claim, 1½ miles south of St. Helens, was acquired about 1846 by Capt. Nathaniel Crosby. With Thomas H. Smith, he began townsite development in 1850. Its few buildings were washed away by a flood in 1861-62.

St. Johns: James Johns took up this claim in 1847. By 1850 some lots had been sold and Johns had a store there. Now part of Portland.

OTHER BOOKS BY EUGENE E. SNYDER

SKIDMORE'S PORTLAND: HIS FOUNTAIN AND ITS SCULPTOR

Victorian Portland, from the 1850s to the 1880s, as seen through the life of Stephen Skidmore. Includes a biography of Olin Warner, the sculptor of Portland's famous Skidmore Fountain.

PORTLAND NAMES AND NEIGHBORHOODS: THEIR HISTORIC ORIGINS

More than 950 street, school, and park names, with biographical information about the persons for whom they are namesakes. Detailed accounts of the development of several noteworthy neighborhoods.

ABOUT THE COVER

The watercolor reproduced on the cover is an original painting done for this book by Newman Myrah, Portland artist. It is the artist's conception of Portland's "Front Street" in 1852, based upon photographs taken in that year.

TO THE READER

BEFORE READING a book, one likes to know something about the author and his intentions. I suppose my interest in Oregon history dates back to a childhood spent amidst the artifacts of "covered-wagon" ancestors. More recently, a professional preoccupation with economic history led me to explore the reasons why some early Oregon towns prospered, while others vanished. I found it to be a story rich in the two ingredients of drama: conflict and heroic characters.

But even more pleasant than knowing a good story is telling it, especially when the material is so dramatic that it needs no fanciful embellishments. I have tried to tell the story of the rivalry among the early townsites along the Willamette within the strict limits of historical accuracy and as personal experiences in the lives of men living at the time. To evoke that sense of reality, I have not resorted to such devices as imagined conversations, but have relied upon quotations from diaries, journals, letters, and the newspapers of the day. The newspaper excerpts help add actuality by the special nineteenth-century flavor of their style.

As I learned the details of the lives and endeavors of those early townsite proprietors, they began to seem like contemporary friends. Their characters came vividly through the years, because they were "Personalities," and rugged ones, each a pillar of individualism. Familiarity did not breed contempt. On the contrary, closer acquaintance added affection to respect for those pioneers. Cynics may call this romanticism, and perhaps it is. Nevertheless, it is the viewpoint which doubtless has influenced my selection and emphasis of material—a useful reminder that no historical writing, however accurate its details, escapes the subjective values of the author.

I have not wished to burden you with cumbersome references, slowing the flow of the narrative by citing the source for every statement made. Wherever possible, I have used primary, first-hand sources contemporary with the events being discussed. In a few cases, there are minor inconsistencies among accounts dealing with the history of this early period. Where some clarification is possible, I have offered explanatory details in footnotes, all of which appear at the end of the book.

Acknowledgments

So many people helped create this book, by their interest, encouragement, suggestions, and assistance, that it would be difficult to list them all. Also, it might be unfair to associate people by name with the manuscript, since ultimate responsibility for decisions as to its style and content lies entirely upon the author.

Special recognition must be given to the Oregon Historical Society. Without the materials accumulated and organized by that great public-spirited institution, this book and others like it could not be written. The Oregon Historical Society made available its collection of old photographs, the source for all of the illustrations appearing in the 16-page picture section. The librarians of the Oregon Historical Society generously helped search out the sometimes elusive facts making up this narrative. The librarians of the Multnomah County Public Library also patiently gave assistance in using their collection of materials concerning Oregon history.

Charles Heaney, Portland artist, did the calligraphy on the maps prepared for this book.

If I were to dedicate this book, it would be to Oregon's pioneer newspapermen. Their style, flamboyant but vigorous, made enjoyable the task of searching their writings for the historical data required for this biography of the early townsites.

Portland, Oregon, December 1970

Second Edition

I'm grateful that the reception of this book warrants this second edition. The text remains about the same—no new facts have come to light to alter the story as originally told. The format has been revised and made more attractive. The photograph of the city in 1983, on the inside cover, was taken by Barry Andrews, Portland photographer.   Eugene E. Snyder

Portland, Oregon, January 1984

Early Portland

Stump-Town
Triumphant

1. THE SETTING

IN JULY 1850, a little steamboat began running between Astoria and Oregon City. If you had just come to Oregon that summer, in response to the reports of its rich land and mild climate, you would have found a trip aboard that steamboat a good way to look over the territory. As you came up the river, you would have stopped at St. Helens, a little clearing with three or four houses and probably a sailing ship at anchor along the river bank. About a mile above St. Helens, you might have seen, up a small inlet, the masts of a sailing vessel taking lumber aboard from the sawmill at the townsite called Milton. You would have had ample time to contemplate the scene, since the steamboat's speed upstream was only four miles per hour. Up the Willamette, you would have seen Linnton, a clearing with a couple of cabins, and, on the opposite side of the river, a cabin marking the beginnings of St. Johns. Another two hours would have brought you to Portland. Here you would have found several dozen neatly-painted white houses, a wharf, perhaps two or three sailing vessels discharging or taking in cargo, and a population of about 400. As you stepped ashore and walked about the village, you would have encountered several men promoting townsites they owned. One visitor to Portland at about this time recorded that almost everyone he met seemed to be promoting a townsite. He heard constantly, "Glad to see you. Hope you will visit my town . . . fifteen

1

houses . . . three houses . . . one shanty . . . and my town-site . . . and mine . . ."

During the years around 1850, there were a dozen townsites along the lower Willamette River. Their owners and promoters were engaged in a great commercial battle to see which location would develop into the territory's principal city. The clearings, cut out of the wilderness, dotted the river bank from Oregon City to St. Helens. Each owner believed, or alleged, that his site was destined to be the metropolis. For the victor, great would be the gains. As for the losers, by-passed by commerce and industry, they would remain quiet villages or disappear completely. Though the rival sites, at the beginning of this drama, were little more than a few acres of stumps surrounded by virgin forest, future fortunes were at stake.

The time was right for townsite promotion. Migration into the Oregon Country was increasing rapidly. After the first wagon train, in 1842, brought about a hundred immigrants to Oregon, 900 came in 1843, 1400 in 1844, and 3000 in 1845. In 1853, overland migration had swelled to 6500. Most of these pioneers were farm families headed for the Willamette Valley, and they were more interested in clearing and working the rich land than speculating in townsites. But also there came, seeking adventure or fortune, the more urban professionals and tradesmen. And among these were enterprising types—strongly motivated optimists who had capital or, if not capital, at least vision and some skill at promotion—who perceived an extraordinary opportunity. They saw that, just as it was "Manifest Destiny" that the United States should extend to the Pacific, it was also the logic of geography that a great port would grow up near the confluence of the Willamette and Columbia rivers. These rivers were deep enough for sea-going vessels to come a hundred miles inland, to take on board the produce of the fertile Willamette and Tualatin valleys, whose increasing population would also provide the necessary market for inbound cargoes of merchandise.

Several riverfront locations seemed to have the potential to become this city. But which site would win out? The rival city fathers chose their favorite sites, laid out their claims, and busily devised schemes to outwit their opponents and turn their own acres into the metropolis of the Oregon Country.

2. TWO WHO WERE TOO SOON

EVEN BEFORE MIGRATION to Oregon had fairly begun, two visionaries had already tried unsuccessfully to establish towns in this area. The first attempt was launched by Hall Kelley in a pamphlet he published at Boston in 1831. Kelley was a schoolteacher who advanced from teaching to writing school books. His books were well received, and from these and other interests, which included surveying and investment in real estate, he became independently wealthy. He used his resources, and indeed exhausted them, in promoting the colonization of Oregon by Americans.

At that time, Oregon was claimed by both Britain and the U.S. Under a joint agreement, nationals of both countries were free to enter, trap for furs, and Christian-

ize Indians. Trade, however, was monopolized by the
Hudson's Bay Company, personified by Dr. John Mc-
Loughlin, the "White-Headed Eagle" at Fort Vancouver. Kelley felt he had a "call" to establish an American colony in Oregon. History does not record what
may have been the cause of his desire to wrest Oregon
from the British. His own ancestors were English. Perhaps the fires of 1776 still smouldered within this de-
scendant of old New England colonists. Whatever the
reason, he became a zealot — some regarded him as a
single-minded fanatic — in advocating, by speeches,
tracts, and letters to Congress, Oregon's colonization.

Kelley had been engaged in this crusade for several
years prior to the publication of his plan of 1831. That
plan called for a great overland trek, by 5000 persons.
They would use wagons, which had not yet been tried
on the plains. Many people did become interested, but
the group never organized. As people got to know
Kelley, they began to have misgivings, not least about
the fact that he had never himself been farther west than
Washington, D.C. Kelley's 1831 pamphlet contained a
neatly drawn diagram for a Christian Utopian community. The townsite would have been located on the
east bank of the Willamette, about where the University
of Portland is today. This was approximately the farthest point up the Willamette reached by members of the
Lewis & Clark Expedition, and Kelley's visions were
based largely on the *Journals* of those explorers. He was
doubtless influenced by this description, by Captain
Clark, of the point to which he ascended the Willamette:

> At this place I think the width of the river may be
> stated at 500 yards, and sufficiently deep for a Man-
> of-War or ship of any burthen.

When his followers gradually backed away from the venture, Kelley decided to come to Oregon anyway, to look over the site he had chosen for his city. He was 42 years old when he left Boston, in November 1832. He stopped first at Washington, D.C., for an unsuccessful attempt to persuade Congress to appropriate money for his expenses. He then travelled via New Orleans and across Mexico, at that time the best established land route to the Pacific. He had made much of the trip alone, or with a Mexican guide. He reached San Diego in April 1834. There, he found companions for the last leg of the trip, some men who were taking horses northward to sell in Oregon. Unfortunately, the Spanish authorities in California had reason to believe that some of the horses had been stolen. The Spanish governor at Monterey sent a message by sailing ship to McLoughlin, informing him that a band of horse thieves were headed for Fort Vancouver.

On his arrival at Fort Vancouver October 15, 1834, Kelley got an unenthusiastic welcome, which was hardly surprising. Besides the dispatch about the stolen horses, McLoughlin had also read Kelley's own writings, which, from the Hudson's Bay Company point of view, could only be regarded as subversive. American colonization would mean Britain's ultimate loss of the country, and extensive agriculture the end of fur trapping. The Company saw Oregon as a vast beaver farm, which, carefully operated on a sustained yield basis, might last indefinitely. Despite these misgivings, the humanitarian McLoughlin took care of Kelley's physical needs, but denied him social intercourse and required him to sleep in a hut outside the stockade.

Kelley spent a winter of discontent along the Columbia. Unaccepted and frustrated, he occasionally visited the clearing, a few miles down the river, where Nathaniel Wyeth was building some log cabins in an attempt to start an American trading post. Wyeth, a fellow New Englander, had reached Fort Vancouver about a month before Kelley. When not trying vainly to interest others in his venture, Kelley was tramping through the underbrush across the river, where his favorite townsite was located.

After five months of this, Kelley headed for home, in defeat. In order to get away, he had, ignominiously, to accept free passage, which McLoughlin enthusiastically provided, on a Hudson's Bay Company vessel. In March 1835, he left the Columbia on board the brig *Dryad*, bound for Hawaii, which then still bore Lord Sandwich's name. He spent six months in the Sandwich Islands. From there, he suffered the further indignity of having to travel home in a whaling ship. Whalers—reeking, dirty, rough and slow—were not the traveller's first choice. The voyage, round Cape Horn, took eleven months, and Kelley reached Boston in September 1836. He was four years older than when he left Boston, possibly wiser, definitely poorer. He had spent his entire fortune, about $30,000, on his Oregon publications, promotions, and trip. That was an immense sum in New England in the 1830s, when skilled laborers were paid $1.50 per day, and the finest Havana cigars cost 2¢ each.

Despite Kelley's belief that he had Divine Inspiration for his venture, his city existed only on paper and had neither building nor name. However, the neatly drawn map, with its rectangular blocks, in his pamphlet of 1831 has a curious similarity to a map of Portland in 1970.

The course of the river was slightly inaccurate—he had only Captain Clark's crude sketch to go by—but there are similarities between his map and that portion of the city today. Perhaps it is only due to Kelley's long run of bad luck (or poor judgment, as many of his contemporaries would have called it) that today's half-million Portlanders are not called Kelleyites.

The second attempt to establish a town in the vicinity of the Lower Willamette was made by Nathaniel Wyeth. A businessman in Boston, Wyeth was originally interested in Oregon by the earlier writings of Kelley. By 1831, Wyeth had concluded that Kelley's expedition was going nowhere, and he decided to organize a party of his own. Disillusioned with Kelley as a practical executive, Wyeth nevertheless had become convinced that Kelley's visions contained a workable idea. However, Wyeth would begin his settlement not with a great migration of families, but with a small nucleus of artisans and mechanics, who would build an outpost from which to engage in trade with the merchants of Boston. His party consisted of his brother, a cousin, and nineteen working-men of various trades.

Wyeth's personality was at the opposite end of the spectrum from Kelley's. Wyeth was a man of vigorous physique and engaging manners, an extrovert and something of a showman. He and his companions prepared for their expedition in grand style, dressing in uniforms and holding drills. Their preparations concluded with a "Wild West Show" in Boston, which they left March 1, 1832. They travelled by ship from Boston to Baltimore, then by the just-completed "Baltimore and Ohio Railroad" to the Ohio River, and thence by river steamer to St. Louis. From Independence, Missouri, a frontier town that was to become the starting point of the Oregon Trail when covered wagons began to roll in the 1840s, they proceeded by pack horse. The expedition was like a holiday lark until they reached the Rocky Mountains, when things became more serious and half of the intrepid adventurers dropped out and returned home.

Wyeth and ten stout-hearted followers reached Fort Vancouver October 24, 1832. There, bad news awaited them. Wyeth had sent a vessel, the *Sultana*, round Cape Horn to meet them at Fort Vancouver, with his heavy supplies. The *Sultana* had left Boston in the fall of 1831, but had been wrecked in the Sandwich Islands, word of which disaster had been brought to Fort Vancouver by a Hudson's Bay Company vessel. Without his materials, Wyeth could not engage in trade or do any building. He and his men spent the winter in the hospitality of McLoughlin. Wyeth, using his time to get to know the territory, decided that his idea had been a good one, though a larger effort, with more resources and men, would be needed for the audacious enterprise of establishing a trading post within the very shadow of Hudson's Bay Company. So he returned, overland, to New England during 1833, and set about organizing a second expedition. Such was his power of persuasion, and his account of the potential opportunities, that he had no difficulty in finding men to accompany him or supply capital. The second expedition also included the dispatch of a vessel, the brig *May Dacre,* to meet the overland portion of the party at Fort Vancouver.

An important addition to Wyeth's second expedition was the Methodist missionary Jason Lee. Lee and his nephew, Daniel Lee, were the first missionaries to reach Oregon. Wyeth allowed Lee to put aboard the *May*

Dacre the freight for the Oregon mission. It included farming implements, tools, household goods, books, garden seed, and live chickens. In April 1834, the Lees, with three lay assistants, joined Wyeth in Missouri. The missionary party, besides the five men, included 10 horses, 4 mules, and 3 cows. Wyeth's party comprised 70 men and 250 head of horses, mules, and cattle. With the missionary group bringing up the rear, the pack train moved out of Independence on April 28, 1834.

Some sidelights on Wyeth, and on life in a pack train of fur trappers and frontiersmen, are contained in letters Jason Lee wrote during the trek. Of Wyeth, Lee wrote: "I would not have it mentioned to his injury, but the Captain is a perfect infidel as it respects revealed religion." ["Captain," a title bestowed upon the leader of a party, was a courtesy usage of the plains, having no military significance. However, force of habit being strong, the title was often retained by these men for years afterwards.] Lee also noted, "We get on fine, but are in the most profane company I was ever in," adding that "the Captain himself indulges in the habit, though he says he is ashamed of it." The combination of devout missionaries and stubborn mules may have posed something of a strain for the Captain and his rough frontiersmen. Incidentally, the Lee party succeeded in driving two of their cows all the way to Fort Walla Walla and thus had fresh milk for the four-month, 1800-mile trip. Along the route, Wyeth and his party stopped to build a fur trading depot, which he named Fort Hall, on the Snake River near present-day Pocatello.

The overland party reached Fort Vancouver in September 1834, within a few days of the arrival of the *May Dacre*, a miraculous coincidence, considering the uncer-

tainties and the technology of that day. The convenient
timing of the two arrivals, if not a proof of Providential
intercession, was at least a great tribute to Wyeth's effi-
ciency and organizational management.

The Wyeth party, as already noted, reached Fort Vancouver about a month before Kelley appeared on the
scene. Thus, Wyeth had made two trips from Boston to
Oregon in little more time than Kelley had taken for one.
Kelley would probably have been more effective if he
had thrown in his fortune and fate with Wyeth. However, original minds tend to be rather independent in
such things, particularly when, as was true of Kelley,
they feel a strong sense of parenthood for the initial idea.

During the fall of 1834, Wyeth set up a trading post
at the northern tip of Wappatoo (later known as Sauvie)
Island. Here, at what is now called Warrior Rock, Wyeth
unloaded the goods from the *May Dacre*. Log huts were
built for the men who had come with him. Wyeth named
the site "Fort William," after one of his partners, and
paced off some hypothetical streets for a town he envis-
aged. The following spring, Wyeth moved his trading
post about 14 miles south, on the west side of Sauvie
Island. The new site was on high ground that would be
safe from most floods. It was just across Multnomah
Channel from the riverbank end of a trail (now called
Logie Trail Road) which led over the hills to the Tualatin Valley. Wyeth sowed wheat on the island. His plan
was to engage in trade with the Indians and settlers, and
to export dried salmon to Boston.

Although Wyeth was a practical Yankee and a good
organizer, his venture did not succeed. The Hudson's
Bay Company had too firm a hold upon trade. "The
Company" had a greater variety of merchandise to offer.

It had well established contacts, and agents at a network of outposts connected by trails of communication. Hudson's Bay Company had, after all, been on the ground for a long time. The initials "HBC" were well known to every Indian and immigrant. Some, indeed, said they actually stood for "Here Before Christ." The Indians hesitated to offend "The Company" by selling or trading their salmon to Wyeth. If Wyeth had had the resources to engage in the triangular trade—New England, Pacific Coast, Orient—that became so profitable in the 1850s, and if the Willamette-Columbia area had developed sufficiently in 1835 to support such a trade, Wyeth might have succeeded. As it was, he turned out to have been wise before the event. The *May Dacre* had to sail, unprofitably, with only half a cargo of salmon. In 1836, Wyeth gave up the enterprise and returned overland to New England. "Fort William" was abandoned. Hudson's Bay Company took over the island for a beef and dairy operation, which was put under the care of a French Canadian called Laurent Sauvé.

With their embryonic townsites, both Kelley and Wyeth were ahead of their time. But the reports of their endeavors added to the growing interest in Oregon, and so helped inspire the later development of the city which their imaginations had foreseen.

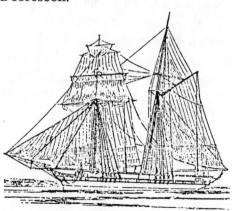

Topsail Coasting Schooner

3. FORT VANCOUVER: NOT A CONTENDER

Seal of the Hudson's Bay Company

SINCE FORT VANCOUVER was well established by the 1830s, and McLoughlin, from his headquarters there, easily defeated Wyeth's challenge, it might have seemed logical to expect that site to grow into the region's principal city. Following its construction in 1825, the post had been, practically speaking, the capital of the Oregon Country, with McLoughlin the country's benign but omnipotent overlord. In the 1830s, it was an active place, with a population of clerks, artisans, servants, and traders numbering as many as 800. From 1825 onward, it had been the port for many ships sent out from England by Hudson's Bay Company and for

"Company" vessels trading with the north Pacific coast, California, and the Sandwich Islands.

For several reasons, however, Fort Vancouver was not a contender in the townsite battle of the 1850s. First of all, it had never been intended by Hudson's Bay Company as a "townsite" for colonization. "The Company" developed only those facilities suitable to an outpost for fur trading. The economy of Fort Vancouver rested upon that single foundation.

Secondly, it was British, not American. As the tide of American colonization made it certain that at least part of the Oregon Country would eventually go to the U.S., with agriculture driving out the beaver, "The Company" began to shift its personnel to British Columbia. It abandoned its "sustained yield" beaver trapping policy south of the Columbia River and began trapping everything possible, almost to extinction, preparatory to pulling its operations out of that part of the Oregon Country. "The Company" established Fort Victoria on Vancouver Island in 1843, to take the place of Fort Vancouver as its main post on the Pacific Coast. The population and importance of Fort Vancouver began to decline. In 1845, McLoughlin resigned from "The Company" and moved to Oregon City. When the American flag went up over Fort Vancouver in August 1846, as a result of the treaty establishing the U.S.-Canadian boundary, Oregon City had already replaced Fort Vancouver as the principal settlement in the Oregon Country.

Its British affiliation had constituted a barrier between Fort Vancouver and the Americans who first came into the Oregon Country. In the case of Wyeth, the barrier was commercial. There was also a kind of social barrier, which, of course, did not apply to men such as

Wyeth or the missionaries. But many of the early Americans who came into Hudson's Bay Company's fur empire were "mountain men" who were or had been
trappers for the rival American Fur Company, and they
had no love for Fort Vancouver. They were generally a
wild and rough crowd who might have been uncomfortable in the relatively restrained atmosphere at McLoughlin's post. The historian Bancroft describes a meeting
of these "mountain men," at a rendezvous in the Rocky
Mountains, as a scene of drinking, carousing, and "the
usual mixture of mirth and murder brooding, of obstrep-
erous jollity, whooping, roaring and wolfish snarling."
By the 1840s, however, the Americans coming into Oregon were colonists, not itinerant mountaineers but stable
settlers, some of whom were well educated gentlemen
from the eastern cities. These new Oregonians were
anti-Vancouver only in the political sense that they
wished the Oregon Country to become part of "the
States."

When Britain sent a naval vessel to Fort Vancouver
to look after British interests during the negotiation of
the international boundary, its officers were welcomed
with open arms and the vessel became a center of gay
social diversions. Her Britannic Majesty's Sloop *Modeste*,
568 tons, 18 guns, arrived at Fort Vancouver in October
1845 and remained till April 1847. During this interval,
the *Spectator*, the Oregon Country's only newspaper,
published every two weeks at Oregon City, contained
many accounts of social affairs involving the gallant officers and men of the *Modeste*. On February 3, 1846, for
example, three comedies were performed aboard the
Modeste, to which many people travelled from as far
away as Oregon City. Their day-long journeys by horse-

back or canoe were tributes to the hospitality of the
Modeste; they also revealed a longing for the amenities
these Oregonians remembered from their homes in the
East. The editor of the *Spectator* was present at one performance and, under the headline "Theatrical Intelli-
gence," wrote a review praising the acting, adding,
"The scenery, painted by themselves, is really beautiful."
On February 19, 1846, "Captain Baillie and the gun-
room officers of the *Modeste* entertained a numerous
circle at a ball." In May, there was a "picnic on the banks
of Vancouver Lake, followed by a ball aboard the
Modeste." In October, the enterprising officers organized
a horse race meet. There was a note of sadness in the
Spectator's report, April 15, 1847, that "H.B.M.S.[1]
Modeste, Captain Baillie, is under sailing orders." The
editor left no doubt that his regrets were sincere:

> We can truly say that Capt. Baillie and his officers
> in leaving our Territory carry with them assurance
> of the high consideration and respect in which they
> are held by a host of friends. The names of many of
> these gentlemen are upon our subscription list,
> where they have been since the first establishment
> of a press in Oregon.

Comparing the recreations of the "mountain men,"
described earlier, with those of the officers of the *Modeste* (acting in drawing-room dramas and painting theatrical scenery), one begins to understand what an
observer meant when he wrote, regarding relations between the early American trappers and the "establishment" at Vancouver: "There could never be congeniality
between persons so entirely dissimilar as an American
frontiersman and a British naval officer."

The affair of the *Modeste* was a final bit of glory for
Fort Vancouver. After the boundary settlement, the

Hudson's Bay Co. continued to maintain a small warehouse there for several years, but in 1849, the U.S. Army began occupying the "Fort," and the old stockade became a military garrison. However, just to the west of the military post, a townsite called "Columbia City" grew up. It was surveyed in August 1850, and its promoter advertised a sale of lots the following month in the *Spectator*. Columbia City, the antecedent of present-day Vancouver, Washington, might have been a contender in the townsite battle, except for one decisive handicap. Few settlers had located in that vicinity, so that it had little developed hinterland to draw upon. The lack of settlers resulted from a deliberate policy of the Hudson's Bay Co. When "The Company" concluded that the Oregon Country south of the Columbia would probably go to the U.S., it had continued to hope that Britain might get the territory to the north of the river. Hence "Company" policy had been to steer settlers, as well as Methodist missionaries, to the Willamette Valley, and to do everything possible to discourage settlement by Americans north of the Columbia. And there was another way in which the boundary question affected the pattern of settlement. It was widely believed, and correctly so as it turned out, that in the portion of the Oregon Country that would become part of the U.S., settlers would receive 640 acres of land free. Bills to provide this were introduced in Congress in 1839-40 by Senator Lewis F. Linn, of Missouri. These bills could not become law at that time since American jurisdiction over Oregon had not yet been established. However, the bills he introduced did more than lead to the grateful immortalization of Linn's name in Linn City, Linnton, and Linn County. The bills also encouraged people to migrate to Oregon in the conviction that eventually they would receive free land. Since it was assumed that, at the least, everything south of the Columbia would go to the U.S., that was where the newcomers settled, beginning with Elijah White's party in 1842. The U.S. government sent White as "Indian Agent" to Oregon. His official title was somewhat misleading, but any title more political in implications would have been inappropriate considering the negotiations going on with Britain over the boundary. But the U.S. government instructed White to take with him as many American settlers as he could. Over a hundred, including many families, accompanied him, most of them settling in or near Oregon City. Once the pattern had been established, prior settlement attracted future settlement, with the result that most of the thousands of immigrants during the 1840s and 1850s chose the Willamette Valley for their homes. An additional factor was that the Willamette Valley and its tributary, the Tualatin Valley, had deep, rich soils of great fertility.

For shipping the wheat and other produce from these farms, a port was needed as close to these valleys as possible, particularly in view of the condition of the roads of the day. Even though Fort Vancouver had excellent navigational facilities, there being no question that any ship that could get over the Columbia River bar could reach Vancouver, it was not accessible to the farmers of the Willamette and Tualatin Valleys. The future great port and city had to be on the Lower Willamette, where ships could meet wagons. Effectively, the possible location was restricted to the stretch of the river between Oregon City and St. Helens. The latter, though facing the Columbia River, may be said to be in the "Lower Willamette" area, since it is at the junction of the lower branch of the Willamette (the slough that flows around Sauvie Island) and the Columbia. Both Kelley's and Wyeth's sites had met this locational requirement; theirs were simply cases of too little and too soon.

4. OREGON CITY'S EARLY ADVANTAGES

Seal of Oregon City in the 1840s

THE FIRST TOWNSITE along the Lower Willamette that did have a future was Oregon City. The location was selected in 1829 by McLoughlin as a site for one of Hudson's Bay Company's trading posts.

It was just at the foot of a spectacular natural Falls in the Willamette, where the river plunges 40 feet over a rocky ledge. There was an Indian village nearby; the cataracts and the pool below the Falls were great places for salmon fishing, and salmon, along with roots and berries, were a staple of the diet of these Indians. However, it was more than a decade after establishment of the trading post before McLoughlin began to think of the location as a townsite. It was not until 1842 that he surveyed it, laid out town lots, and gave it its name.

At the time, there were several other small settlements on the Willamette—Champoeg, French Prairie, the mission station at Chemeketa—but they were all above the Falls. And even the most persuasive townsite promoter could not conjure up a vision of ocean vessels climbing over the Falls. Oregon City was not only below the Falls but, of the scattered settlements along the Willamette, it was the most town-like.

In the summer of 1840, "The Falls," as the Oregon City site was called, had been the scene of two attempts to breach Hudson's Bay Company's trade monopoly. The first was not successful. It was the visit to the Willamette River by Capt. John Couch, in the brig *Maryland*. The Pacific Northwest was beginning to attract the attention of the great merchant trading houses of New England and New York. Couch was sent out by Cushing & Co., of Newburyport, Mass., to trade in the Sandwich Islands and Oregon. He hoped to trade for salmon in Oregon, and exchange the salmon in Oahu for goods, such as hides, tallow and whale oil, to take back to New England. Couch had been a sailor since he was 15; he was 28 when he was given command of the *Maryland*. He was a skillful pilot, and managed, without charts, to bring his vessel not only into the Willamette but right up to "The Falls." This feat was possible because the Willamette was very high, due to backwater from the June flood in the Columbia River. Trading, however, proved to be even more difficult than navigation. Just as Wyeth before him, Couch found it hard to persuade the Indians to fish for anyone other than "The Company." He did a little trading, using his vessel as his store. Then, fearing that lower water would make the river unnavigable, he brought the *Maryland* downstream and sailed for Honolulu. There, since the trading plan had not worked, Couch sold the *Maryland* at a good price, and went home on another vessel.

At the time the *Maryland* went down the river, in June 1840, another American vessel, the ship *Lausanne*, 400 tons, had just arrived at Fort Vancouver, with a "Great Reinforcement" of Methodist missionaries to join Jason Lee. It brought 51 persons, including wives and children. In distributing this group, Lee assigned Rev. Alvin Waller, with his wife and two children, to "The Falls." There, late in the summer of 1840, Rev. Waller built a house, which served as a residence and also as a mission store. This store, at first stocked with very limited supplies, survived and grew into a successful competitor against Hudson's Bay Company, particularly under the later management of George Abernethy. The Methodists' missionary activities along the Willamette were closed out about 1844. The lackadaisical Indians of the Willamette Valley—those who survived the epidemics—had proved indifferent to the blessings, either spiritual or temporal, of civilization—with one possible exception: liquor, or "Blue Ruin"[13] as it was called. As for the immigrants, they were being ministered to by newly organized churches. So the missions were phased out. The mission store at Oregon City was taken over by George Abernethy as a purely secular operation. Abernethy was one of the missionaries who had come out in the *Lausanne* in 1840. Born in Scotland and trained in New York City, Abernethy was an ardent Methodist, but he did not find religion an impediment to a successful business and political career. As the fortunes of Hudson's Bay Company declined, those of Abernethy rose. He developed a profitable trade with Hawaii, exporting wheat and salmon in exchange for sugar and molasses. And he imported entire shiploads of manufactured goods from the East Coast, round Cape Horn. Abernethy was also elected Governor of Oregon when provisional government was first organized, in July 1845.

Meanwhile, Capt. Couch, having arrived back at Newburyport early in 1841, had been describing the territory and trade problems to Cushing. They decided to try again. In the brig *Chenamus*, named for an Indian chief living near Astoria whom Couch had met on his previous visit, he came back to the Willamette in June 1842. This time, despite his skill and experience, he was only able to reach the "Clackamas Rapids," about two miles downstream from "The Falls." Anchored just below the rapids, he unloaded his goods into canoes, to take them on to Oregon City, where he opened an "American Store." This time, the plan of attack was a bit different. Convinced that there was no profit in trying to barter with the Indians, whose trade was so closely tied to "The Company," Cushing and Couch decided to try to sell to the white settlers, whose numbers were few but increasing. Couch's store was to be in the Yankee tradition, an informal lounging place for gossip, where an easy equality prevailed, and where American settlers would find familiar American goods. By contrast, Hudson's Bay Company operated in the more formal tradition of the British. Their store was efficient, but there was little socializing; the purchaser presented a requisition at a narrow little window, the goods were quickly handed out, and the man at once vacated to make room for the next in line.

After unloading his goods, Couch brought the *Chenamus* down the river, to a safer anchorage just below Ross Island, and returned by canoe to Oregon City, to build a cabin for his store. In the fall of 1842, leaving his store in charge of Mr. A. E. Wilson, Couch sailed for New England. Thus, by the summer of 1842, there were at Oregon City two American stores challenging Hudson's Bay Company—Couch's and the Methodist mission's.

Three months after Couch's arrival in the *Chenamus*, Oregon City was further Americanized when Elijah White's party of about a hundred immigrants arrived from "the States." This was the first wagon train of settlers to come to Oregon, the few previous immigrants having come by pack horse or by ship. Actually, the White party brought their wagons only as far as Fort Hall, in southeastern Idaho. From there, they used pack horses. They arrived at Oregon City in September 1842. This was Oregon's first real colony of Americans, other than the Methodist missionary headquarters near present-day Salem. White's party included several men who became important in the development of the territory. Among them were A. L. Lovejoy, one of the founders of the Portland townsite, and Hugh Burns, founder of a rival townsite called "Multnomah City," across the river from Oregon City. Another member of the White party was Sidney Moss, a man of divers parts, originally a stone mason, who became Oregon's first hotel keeper and "licensed retailer of spiritous liquors" and who, the year after his arrival on this remote frontier, organized "The Falls Debating Society." Moss later recalled that, when the White party arrived, there were sixteen men living at Oregon City. He was not counting women or Indians. There was at least one woman, the wife of Rev. Waller, of the Methodist mission. And there were numerous Indians, especially when the fishing was good. In September 1842, there were only four buildings at Oregon City. One was a frame structure, the Methodist mission and store. The other three were log cabins. One of these was the Hudson's Bay Company trading post and another was Couch's store. The third belonged to some Americans—"claim-jumpers" in the view of Mc-Loughlin — who were building a sawmill there. The White party not only Americanized Oregon City, but increased its population many fold. During the winter of 1842-43, the number of buildings increased from four to thirty.

In 1843, another merchant arrived at Oregon City, a man of special importance to our story because he later became the first active developer of the Portland townsite—Francis W. Pettygrove. Born in Maine in 1812, Pettygrove was a clerk for the New York City merchant house, Benson & Bros., at the time they decided to enter the Oregon trade. Pettygrove was selected for the assignment, a wise choice as it turned out. Accompanied by his wife and children, he left New York City in March 1842 in the ship *Victoria*, with $15,000 worth of goods. After a voyage of seven months, round Cape Horn, they reached Honolulu in October 1842, where they had to wait six months for a vessel to bring them to Oregon. They finally found passage on a small bark, the *Fama*, and, early in May 1843, reached Fort Vancouver. From there, they came up to Oregon City in a little river-sized schooner, arriving May 19, 1843, and Pettygrove opened a well-stocked store.

Since there was little money in circulation, most trade at this time was on a barter basis. Pettygrove began to trade his goods for furs, with the idea of shipping the furs to New York. When McLoughlin heard of this, he came up from Fort Vancouver by canoe, to pay Pettygrove a visit, informing him that Hudson's Bay Company had a monopoly on the fur trade. Pettygrove refused to back down, however, saying he was within his rights as an American citizen under the joint occupation treaty, as indeed he was. So, to maintain his monopoly, McLoughlin offered to buy all the furs Pettygrove collected, paying more than Pettygrove could get by shipping them to New York. Pettygrove did ship lumber, flour, and salmon to Hawaii, where they were traded for other goods more valuable in New York.

With its four stores and sawmill, Oregon City in 1843 had a good headstart on later townsites along the Lower Willamette, and for several years it maintained its early lead. The notable feature of its site, the Falls in the river, was a great asset. The Willamette was the region's main artery for movement of goods and people, and the portage necessary at "The Falls," as the town continued to be known colloquially, made it a transportation center. It was a one-night stop for river traffic, which consisted mostly of canoes and bateaux. A bateau, given its name by the French Canadians who were so important in Hudson's Bay Company's fur empire, was a flat-bottomed boat with a sharp bow. It was propelled by Indians hired to paddle it—or drag it by ropes from the shore.

Another benefit from the Falls was that the river's drop at that point provided water power. The sawmill which began operating there in 1842 was soon followed by other mills. By 1847, Oregon City was described as "a beautiful, bustling little village, with its neatly-painted white houses, its 600 inhabitants, the noise of two flour mills and two sawmills, and the Babel of English, American, Kanaka (Hawaiian), and Indian."

An important contributor to this growth at Oregon City was McLoughlin himself. Because of differences over policy, which a trip to London during 1838-39 had not resolved, McLoughlin resigned from the Hudson's Bay Company in 1845 and moved to Oregon City. In 1846, he built the "McLoughlin House," maintained today in its original style as a monument and museum. By 1846, he had also built a sawmill and flour mill at Oregon City. At 61, McLoughlin was still energetic and adaptable. His commitment to his new home was complete. His son David, who returned to Oregon about this time from England, where he had been to school, went to work with Pettygrove. Dr. McLoughlin even became a U.S. citizen, in 1851, and in that year was elected mayor of Oregon City, receiving 44 votes, to 22 for his opponent. (The surprisingly small number of votes cast is a reminder that only adult male property-owners voted in local elections in those days.)

With the stimulus given to its growth by its mills and stores, Oregon City became the Territory's political headquarters. It was designated the capital when provisional government was organized, in 1845. Culture, too, followed commerce. In 1843, the "Pioneer Lyceum and Literary Club" was formed at Oregon City, and a circulating library was established by donations of a few books. Within four years, that public library had grown to "300 well-selected volumes." In 1846, the *Spectator*, the Oregon Country's first newspaper, and indeed the first newspaper on the Pacific Coast, began publication, every other Thursday, at Oregon City. In that year, the town was reported to contain "two churches and one tavern," a surprising inversion of what is usually considered the normal ratio in pioneer communities, due doubtless to the influence of Methodism. By 1847, Oregon City had "one day-school and one female boarding school, in which are taught all the branches usually comprised in a thorough English education, together with plain and ornamental needle-work, drawing, and painting in mezzotinto and water-colors."

Clearly, Oregon City was on the move. But, despite these impressive beginnings, Oregon City faced an insurmountable obstacle in the contest to become the Oregon metropolis. It was practically inaccessible to ocean-going vessels. The major barrier was the "Clackamas Rapids," a gravel bar and shoals about two miles downstream from Oregon City, created by the Clackamas River as it enters the Willamette. The flour and lumber from Oregon City's mills had to be "bateaued" down the river and loaded onto ocean vessels at some point downstream.

Bark

5. RIVAL TOWNSITES AT THE FALLS

THE CLACKAMAS RAPIDS ruled out a metropolitan future not only for Oregon City but also for two rival townsites on the opposite bank of the Willamette. The first of these was begun by Robert Moore, a pioneer from Illinois and Missouri, who arrived in Oregon in 1840. In the spring of 1841, Moore "purchased" a square mile of land, encompassing the entire west bank of the river facing the Falls, from an old Indian chief in exchange for some goods. He also claimed it under the free-land bill introduced in Congress by Senator Linn in 1840, but which did not become law for a decade. In 1841, up on the hillside, Moore built a log cabin and called the site "Robin's Nest." The following year, about the same time McLoughlin laid out Oregon City, Moore marked off lots on his claim. Moore changed his townsite's name to the less poetic but more dignified "Linn City," in honor of his favorite senator. When the White party arrived, in September 1842, the first question Moore asked was, "Has Linn's bill passed?"

The other rival neighbor to Oregon City was established by Hugh Burns, who came with the White party. He claimed the square mile just to the north of Moore's, and called his site "Multnomah City." By 1844, both Moore and Burns had "public ferries" (they were canoes) operating between their townsites and Oregon City. The *Spectator*, in 1846, reported that Linn City contained a tavern, chair manufacturer, cabinet shop, gunsmith, and wagon shop. At Multnomah City, however, there was not much action. In 1846, the *Spectator* said of Multnomah City: "It is located on a beautiful site and must, in a short time, be a city in appearance as well as name."

In 1851, Moore tried to promote some industrial development on his side of the river with this advertisement in the *Spectator*:

RARE CHANCE FOR INVESTMENT

THE undersigned, being proprietor of one of the finest water powers in the world, would propose to have the same improved. He will offer such inducements to those desirous of engaging in such an enterprise that they can not fail to meet their views. Said water power is situated at the Great Falls of the Willamette.

Robert Moore

Linn City

Regardless of the rivalry between Oregon City and its two satellites—a rivalry more quixotic than substantive—they were all thwarted by the same fate, in the form of the Clackamas Rapids. It was true that a few small sailing vessels, during the 1840s and 1850s, reached Oregon City, to the great joy of the upstream town proprietors. But it was feasible to sail over the Rapids only when a flood in the Columbia backed water up the Willamette to the Falls, making the Willamette temporarily a deep lake. That had been the condition when, in the spring of 1840, Couch brought the *Maryland* up to the Falls. However, a great ocean port could not grow upon such a tenuous and treacherous channel. Even the Oregon City merchants Abernethy and Pettygrove, who were engaged in trade with Hawaii and New York, could only expect to bring their vessels up to the Clackamas Rapids. Normally, the vessels stopped much farther down and the goods were trans-shipped by bateau. Up to the mid-

1840s, their usual terminus was Fort Vancouver. Thereafter, they began coming to anchor at the various townsites that were developing along the Lower Willamette.

Today, with a century of hindsight, we can clearly see that Oregon City could not have become an ocean port. It was less obvious to the proprietors, merchants, and editors of that community in the 1840s. For several years, they argued bravely about the town's port possibilities. It was part of a vehement and bitter controversy among the rival townsites as to who possessed that elusive but all-important feature, the "Head of Navigation." This became a matter of great concern about 1850. But, at Oregon City, though there were many words about ships, few ships were ever seen.

The Clackamas Rapids were not the only obstacle in the river. In 1842, when Captain Couch had found it impossible to get the *Chenamus* over the Rapids, even though he had timed his arrival to coincide with the high water of June, he had anchored just below the Rapids to unload his cargo. But even that temporary anchorage was uncomfortable because, farther downstream, at Ross Island, was a bar that became dangerous at low water. And the river would fall after the June freshet. Fearing that he might be trapped in the upper river, Couch had turned the *Chenamus* around and brought it eleven miles downstream, below Ross Island, to an uninhabited clearing which later was to become "Portland." It was a site he carefully noted, as being one to which he could bring sailing vessels with safety during most of the year.

6. THE FLOURISHING VILLAGE OF PORTLAND

THE FUTURE TOWNSITE of Portland, as seen by Captain Couch in 1842, had not so much as a cabin on it.[2] The clearing on the riverbank there, consisting of about an acre from which the brush had been cut away and burned, had been made by Indians and trappers travelling between the two Hudson's Bay Company posts at Fort Vancouver and Oregon City. They found the site a convenient camp spot, about half-way between the two posts, which were 30 miles apart by river. It was a recognized halt for a mid-day rest and was known, aptly, as "The Clearing." McLoughlin had stopped there many times on his trips up and down the Willamette. Gathering wood for campfires kept the site clear.

The first person to look upon "The Clearing" with a possessive eye (the idea of "owning" real estate had not occurred to the nomadic Indians) was William Overton, a pioneer from Tennessee who came to Oregon in 1841. He worked at the Methodist mission at The Dalles for a few months. (That mission was a branch established by Jason Lee from his headquarters near Salem.) In 1842, Overton made a voyage to Honolulu, at that time the major port serving America's West Coast. In 1843, he was back in Oregon and, with most of the new immigrants staking out claims, he decided "The Clearing" would be a good one. He had it in mind for his claim when, one day in November 1843, he made the canoe trip from Fort Vancouver to Oregon City. Those canoes were large, carrying two or three passengers and their baggage, and propelled by four Indians, who were paid with a woolen shirt or blanket. In the canoe with Overton was Asa Lawrence Lovejoy, a lawyer at Oregon City. When they stepped ashore at "The Clearing" for their mid-day rest, Overton told Lovejoy he wanted to file a claim on "The Clearing." All of the early settlers were assuming that Senator Linn's bill, granting immigrants to Oregon 640 acres of free land, would become law. Pending enactment of that law, the Provisional Government at Oregon City had set up a procedure for recording the settlers' claims. Overton offered Lovejoy one-half the claim if he would take care of the legal paper-work and pay the filing fee, which was 25¢. Lovejoy agreed, and the claim was filed early in 1844. Lovejoy thus acquired a half-interest in what later became the central business district of Portland, for an outlay of 25¢.

As spring came, in 1844, Overton, with the restless disposition of frontiersmen, began to feel the urge to "move on," rather than settle down to the mundane and confining task of developing his acreage. But he was destitute, except for his half-interest in 640 acres of wilderness. That interest he offered to barter to F. W. Pettygrove, the Oregon City merchant, for $50 worth of clothes, equipment, and food, to enable him to strike out for California. The price of $50 was a dramatic mark-up from the 25¢ which the other half of the claim had cost Lovejoy. Nevertheless, in the light of later developments, it was still an attractive, even marvelous, opportunity. But, on the frontier of 1844, $50 was a lot of money. And it was for good reason that Benson & Bros. had selected Pettygrove to look after their trading affairs in Oregon. Before he would accept Overton's offer,

Pettygrove made a thorough investigation of the Overton site. He hired a crew of Indians and, in a canoe, came down the Willamette to its mouth, carefully sounding its depth. He concluded that vessels of the size then in the Oregon trade could easily ascend the Willamette to "The Clearing." This was of great interest to him. The vessels then handling his imports and exports were stopping at Fort Vancouver, since Oregon City was inaccessible and there was no other point along the Willamette with a wharf or warehouse. Satisfied by his investigation, the Yankee trader concluded the deal with Overton, who, properly outfitted, disappeared in the direction of California, and "The Clearing" became the joint property of Lovejoy and Pettygrove.

Later in 1844, Lovejoy and Pettygrove hired a man to cut some trees at their claim, to enlarge the clearing, and to build a cabin. The log cabin built during the winter of 1844-45 and occupied by their employee was the first building at "The Clearing." Early in 1845, the proprietors were beginning to think of their claim as a "townsite." However, it had no name. Lovejoy, from Massachusetts and a graduate of Amherst, wanted to call it "Boston." Pettygrove, the successful merchant from Maine, wanted to name it after the principal city in his state, "Portland." Argument and reasoning proving inconclusive, they decided to fall back upon chance: a large copper penny which Pettygrove had brought from home as a souvenir was flipped, Pettygrove won the toss, and "The Clearing" became "Portland." The coin used on this fateful occasion is now in the possession of the Oregon Historical Society.

During the summer of 1845, the proprietors hired a surveyor, Thomas Brown, who had come across the plains with the immigration of 1843, to lay out a grid of 16 blocks. This original townsite extended from the river to Second and from Washington to Jefferson Streets. They ordered Brown to make the blocks 200 feet square and the streets 60 feet wide, never imagining what such numerous intersections and narrow streets would mean in terms of traffic congestion a century later. The lots were, as they are today in most of the city, 50 x 100 feet. Lots were sold at low prices, or even given away if the recipient would agree to put up a cabin.

In October 1845, the American bark *Toulon*, with Nathaniel Crosby, Jr. as master, arrived in the Columbia River. The *Toulon* brought a new stock of goods for Pettygrove. She also introduced a dramatic innovation: she did not discharge her cargo at Fort Vancouver but came up to the new townsite called Portland, where Pettygrove was building a warehouse. From there, part of the goods were taken by bateau to Oregon City, for Pettygrove's store there. But the rest of the goods were left at the Portland warehouse, which also began serving as a retail store, the first business operation at Portland. Pettygrove had an advertisement in the first issue of the Oregon City *Spectator*, February 5, 1846, announcing that goods "Just Arrived from New York" on the bark *Toulon* were for sale at Oregon City "and at Portland, 12 miles below this City." Portland was still a relatively unknown upstart whose location had to be identified with reference to Oregon City.

Pettygrove took the lead in developing and promoting Portland. Lovejoy was a relatively inactive co-owner whose principal interests were at Oregon City. Lovejoy, after having retained his half-interest in the Portland site for less than two years, sold it, in November 1845, to

Benjamin Stark, who had just arrived as cargomaster on the *Toulon*. Stark paid Lovejoy $1215 for the half-interest in the Portland townsite, plus Lovejoy's half-interest in a "band of cattle" he and Pettygrove had running on the property of Joseph Gale in the Tualatin Valley. The "band of cattle" numbered 110 head, so that Lovejoy's portion, acquired by Stark, was equivalent to 55 head. Records of the 1840s show that the value of cattle varied widely, though prices were clearly going up during the decade. In 1843, "wild cattle" were valued at $10 each, "California cows" at $15-20, and "American cows" at $60-70 each. By 1845, "American cows" were $75-100 each, and other prices appear to have risen proportionately. If we use $15 per head as a fair estimate of the value of Lovejoy's cattle, Stark paid about $825 for the cattle and about $390 for the half-interest in the Portland townsite. Thus, already, the Portland land claim had begun to appreciate in value. A half-interest had changed hands at these prices:

> 1843: Overton to Lovejoy, 25¢
> 1844: Overton to Pettygrove, $50
> 1845: Lovejoy to Stark, $390

And, of course, this was only the beginning of the story.

Lovejoy continued to practice law. In 1846, he was elected mayor of Oregon City, and he was also elected Speaker of the House of Representatives, which met at Oregon City in December 1846. As for Stark, he stayed with the *Toulon* as cargomaster. The *Toulon* remained in the river from October 1845 until February 1846, when she sailed out with a cargo of agricultural produce Pettygrove was sending to the Sandwich Islands. She was back from Oahu, at Pettygrove's warehouse, early in June 1846. Stark was fully occupied as cargomaster and shipping agent, and his purchase of the half-interest in the Portland townsite was a speculative investment rather than a proprietorship; he played no substantial role in developing the town. During the formative years 1845-48, Pettygrove was the active proprietor and developer. Portland's Pettygrove Period laid the foundation for its later success in defeating its rivals.

7. PORTLAND'S PETTYGROVE PERIOD

PETTYGROVE'S PORTLAND warehouse and store were at the foot of Washington Street. The store was managed by George Bell, whose wife was the first white woman to live at Portland. To facilitate handling goods between ships and his warehouse, Pettygrove had hired John Waymire to build a wharf, which was also at the foot of Washington Street. This wharf was sufficiently completed in the summer of 1846 to be used by the *Toulon* when she returned from Oahu in July. Encouraged by the outlook at Portland, Pettygrove decided to make it his residence. He hired John Morrison, a carpenter and a naturalized Scot who had come overland from "the States" in 1842 with Elijah White, to build a house for him. This was the first frame house built in Portland. Pettygrove moved his family there from Oregon City in 1846. The Portland store now became his principal one, with that at Oregon City only a branch. Morrison also built himself a house at the foot of the street named for him.

During 1845-46, Pettygrove opened a wagon route, near present-day Burnside Road, from Portland over the hills to the Tualatin Valley. He also opened a wagon route along the bank of the Willamette from Portland to Oregon City. This latter road was less crucially important than the one to the farms of the Tualatin Plains, however, because, between Portland and Oregon City, river transport was also available.

In the spring of 1846, Pettygrove sold several blocks and lots to men who commenced improvements by putting up log cabins. Among the enterprising immigrants who were sufficiently impressed with the nucleus begun by Pettygrove to throw in their lot with Portland was Daniel Lownsdale. He arrived in December 1845 and took up, as his claim, the square mile just to the west of the Pettygrove-Stark claim. Lownsdale was born in Kentucky, of an old Southern family, and had had a liberal education and business experience before he came to Oregon, at the age of 43. He had been travelling in Europe during the years 1842-44. He was a tanner by trade. In 1846, he built a tannery, located where the Multnomah Civic Stadium now stands. His tannery was on the bank of a creek which came to be known as "Tanner Creek." Lownsdale placed this advertisement in the *Spectator*:

> PORTLAND TANNERY
> This establishment is situated in the midst of plenty of hemlock, the only good tanbark which can be procured in the Territory.
>
> D. H. Lownsdale

Also in 1846, Portland's first blacksmith shop was established, by James Terwilliger. His shop and house were on Morrison Street, between First and Second. He also took up a claim on a square mile of land south of the Portland townsite. Terwilliger's claim was separated from the Pettygrove-Stark claim by an intervening square mile claimed by Elizabeth Caruthers and her son Finice Caruthers, her one and only child.

A picturesque description of Portland in 1846 is contained in a report by Lt. Neil Howison, of the U.S. Navy Schooner *Shark*. He was sent to the Columbia River at the same time H.B.M.S. *Modeste* was at Fort Vancouver, during the international boundary negotiations. U.S.S. *Shark* arrived in the Columbia in July 1846, from the Sandwich Islands, and remained till September 1846. During that summer, Lt. Howison visited Portland and made these observations:

"It has been named Portland by the individual under whose auspices is has come into existence, and mainly to whose efforts its growth and increase are to be ascribed. This is Mr. F. W. Pettygrove, from Maine, who came out here some years back as agent for the mercantile house of Messrs. Benson, of New York. He is now the principal commercial man in the country. He selected Portland as the site of a town accessible to shipping, built houses, and established himself there; invited others to settle around him, and appropriated his little capital to opening wagon roads (aided by neighboring farmers) into Twality Plains, and up the east side of the river to the Falls. Twelve or 15 new houses are already occupied, and others building; and, with a population of more than 60 souls, its prospects of increase are favorable. A good wharf, at which vessels may lie and discharge or take in cargo most months of the year, is also among the improvements of Portland."

With these developments in 1846, Portland began a growth which startled people at other townsites. The editor of the *Spectator* commented in April 1847:

The town of Portland has increased rapidly and surprisingly within the past six months. Its enterprising proprietor [Pettygrove] has built a wharf and a large, commodious warehouse, which, owing

to the place being situated at the head of navigation, will greatly facilitate commercial operations.
There are some pleasant residences there already.
There are many natural advantages in favor of Portland as a point both of residence and business.

This editorial pronouncement, that Portland was the
"head of navigation," annoyed the promoters of rival
townsites. But the opinion was consistent with that of
Captain Couch, who had, in 1840 and again in 1842,
noted "The Clearing" as a place to which he could safely
bring sailing vessels. Couch and his influence played an
important role in promoting Portland. Earlier, Couch
had given a boost to Oregon City by locating his store
there. Now, he stimulated Portland's growth by telling
his many acquaintances among sea captains that Portland was the "head of navigation" on the Willamette.

Couch had sailed out of the Columbia in the *Chenamus* in September 1842, to return to New England. Back
in Newburyport, he and Cushing put together another
cargo for the Oregon trade. Couch, still in command of
the *Chenamus*, left Newburyport September 16, 1843,
again bound for Oahu and Oregon. The log of this trip
contains interesting notes on the voyage. The route
around Cape Horn was always something of a race
against time and previous records, and Captain Couch
was able to write that "We have gained 9 days on the
Maryland's passage and 4 days on the *Chenamus's* last
voyage." Touching at Oahu, he left there "with a large
lot of passengers," who were "sick as death" during the
crossing to the mouth of the Columbia, which they
reached April 22, 1844. This time, Couch arrived earlier
in the season than on his previous two voyages. The
annual spring flood, resulting from melting snow, was
still a month away. With the rivers lower than on his

previous arrivals, Couch brought the *Chenamus* only to the mouth of the Willamette, thinking it prudent not to venture up to "The Clearing." This suggested that Portland might not be readily accessible at all times of the year, a fact, or alleged fact, that was to assume dramatic importance in the coming contest between Portland and St. Helens. Couch "bateaued" his goods to his Oregon City store. This time, however, he decided to remain there himself. He turned the *Chenamus* over to Captain Sylvester, who made several voyages between the Willamette and the Sandwich Islands during 1844-45, before leaving the Pacific Coast.

Couch remained at Oregon City, to become a landsman and one of the leading citizens of that city and, later, of Portland. In March 1846, he was appointed by Governor Abernethy as Treasurer of the Provisional Government, and he was elected to that office in December 1846. He was also a director of the Printing Association that published the *Spectator*. And he continued to operate his store at Oregon City and to receive shipments from New England. Since these shipments had to be transferred to canoes or barges at some point down the river, Couch had many occasions to think of the superior navigational facilities at Portland. Even if the river below Portland might have shallow bars at very low water, it was possible to reach Portland with ease during most of the year. In 1845, Couch took up a land claim there himself, the square mile just to the north of the Pettygrove-Stark claim, which later became "Couch's Addition" to Portland. His claim was recorded in the Territorial Records on August 24, 1845.

Across the river from Pettygrove and Stark, James Stephens had, in 1845, acquired the claim to a square

mile that later became "East Portland." Stephens bought
it for $200 from Dr. McLoughlin, who was administrator
of the estate of a former Hudson's Bay Company employee who had originally claimed it. Thus, by 1846, the
land in the vicinity of the Portland townsite was held by
the following claimants:

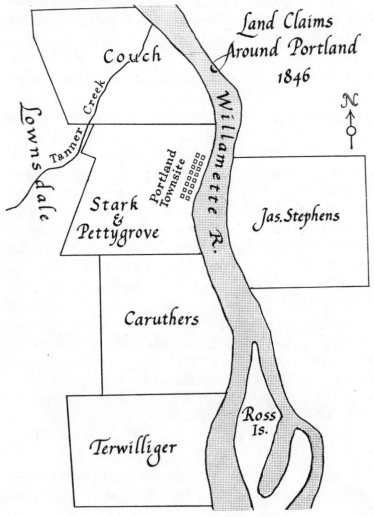

Pettygrove's foresight in quickly getting a wharf built was of great importance to Portland's early growth. An increasing number of vessels were coming to Oregon, and they found that wharf a convenient terminus. A frequent visitor was the *Toulon,* under Captain Crosby. After arriving in the Willamette from New England in October 1845 with goods for Pettygrove, Captain Crosby used the *Toulon* for about four years in a triangular trade between Oregon, Hawaii, and San Francisco. It was the *Toulon* which, arriving at Portland about the 1st of November 1846, on a trip back from Honolulu, brought the first news of the settlement of the Oregon boundary by the U.S. and Britain. The event had actually taken place three months earlier, but news travelled only at the speed of sail. This was the occasion of the first "Extra" published by the *Spectator,* November 4, 1846. Characteristic of the restrained style of the day, however, was the small heading over this dramatic announcement, which simply stated: "Highly Important News." It was an intriguing caption which required the reader to get into the fine print to find out what had happened. In appreciation of the *Toulon's* role in bringing the news, the *Spectator* shortly thereafter printed a eulogy to the vessel, which was still at Portland. This was the editor's "news item":

> The neat and trim bark *Toulon,* Capt. N. Crosby, Jr., is now safely moored alongside the wharf at Portland, receiving cargo. She will soon make her departure for California. The *Toulon* is a "crack" ship, and her officers gentlemanly and efficient.

Captain Crosby appreciated, of course, how welcome to Oregonians would be the news he was bringing about the boundary settlement. As a result, that particular roundtrip between Portland and Honolulu was made in record time—35 days. On the east-bound leg of the voyage, with the exciting news, he had crowded on all the sail the *Toulon* would carry.

With Pettygrove's enterprise, Couch's vote of confidence, and the energy and capital brought by new arrivals such as Lownsdale, Portland's growth accelerated. Its population nearly doubled from 1846 to 1847—from "60 souls" to "about 100." In 1847, a year after Lt. Howison's report, another interesting description of the townsite was given by J. Q. Thornton, an early judge in Oregon under the Provisional Government. Thornton was making a trip back to the East Coast, and his account also shows what travel along the Willamette was like in October 1847. He and his party left Oregon City early in the morning in a gig (a light, fast row boat), rowed by Indians, and reached Portland after 2½ hours. There, they boarded the bark *Whiton*, tied up at Pettygrove's wharf. The trip down to Astoria required several days. Then they had to wait for calm weather to get over the bar, so that they did not sail out of the Columbia until the 17th day after leaving Oregon City. While at Portland, Thornton made these observations:

"Ships drawing 12 or 14 feet can ascend the Wilhamette [one of many early variants in the spelling of this name] to the pleasant and flourishing village of Portland. Vessels could ascend higher, but they cast anchor at Portland because there are warehouses and a convenient wharf at that place. Portland is a small and beautiful village. It contains about 100 inhabitants and has an air of neatness, thrift, and industry."

Contributing to Portland's air of neatness and beauty was a frame house built for Captain Nathaniel Crosby, Jr. His house at Portland was an early version of "prefab" construction. Its components were all cut and marked, ready for assembly, in Boston, and shipped to Honolulu. There, Crosby took them aboard the *Toulon* and brought them to Portland, on the next trip after that on which he had conveyed the news of the boundary settlement. In April 1847, the *Spectator* reported that "One of the most handsome and comfortable dwelling houses in the Territory is now in course of erection at Portland by Messrs. Robb and Morrison for Captain Crosby." No nails were used in putting the house together, only wooden pegs, and all the joints were carefully mortised. The house was in the Cape Cod style, and for many years was a showpiece of Portland.

Though in some ways Portland's appearance was pleasing, it had one feature which incited criticism and ridicule: stumps in its streets. A visitor in 1847 noted that "The trees are cut down where the streets have been surveyed, but the stumps are left." He also observed that the forest came right down to Second Street, though there were "two or three small cabins under the big trees on Third Street." The trees were cut, of course, as building expanded westward, but the stumps remained in many of the streets for several years. Proprietors of rival townsites claimed Portland had more stumps than people and gave it the derisive nickname "Little Stumptown."

In August 1848, the first news of the discovery of gold in California reached Oregon, and it awakened restless stirrings in everyone, including Mr. Pettygrove. In September 1848, Pettygrove sold his half-interest in the square mile containing the Portland townsite to the tanner Lownsdale, who paid him in leather—$5000 worth. During the winter, Pettygrove liquidated his other assets, including his stores, warehouses, wharf, and merchandise, and, in the spring of 1849, left with his family for San Francisco. The principal asset he had brought with him to Oregon City in 1843 consisted of the right to share in the profits on the $15,000 worth of goods his employers had sent out with him. Now, six years later, he had built up a personal fortune of $75,000. That was an impressive capital gain, especially in terms of the level of prices in Oregon during the "Pettygrove Period." Common laborers earned $1.50 a day, skilled laborers $3 a day, beef sold for 7¢ a pound, a "Good Meal" cost 25¢, and 24-hour rental of a horse (a sort of U-Ride) was 75¢. The fortune Pettygrove amassed in six years showed what an enterprising person could do in a frontier environment. Pettygrove said, in an interview many years later concerning his merchandising days on the Willamette, "I got a large majority of the trade during my stay there."

He also did well with exports. Pettygrove and the ship captains who carried his goods could make good profits on goods both coming and going. It was, of course, very expensive to bring manufactured goods to Oregon. But prices were marked up to cover that. In 1847, Waymire, who had built Pettygrove's wharf for him, was complaining that he had had to pay Pettygrove $2.50 for six cups and saucers "which could be had in the States for 25¢." And then the outbound cargo brought a nice profit, too. In 1847, even before the "Gold Rush" had made Oregon produce worth almost its weight in gold, a barrel of flour could be bought on the Willamette for $6 and sold in San Francisco for $15. Comparable profits could be made on lumber. Exports from Oregon are illustrated by those of a typical month:

April 1847. During that month, the following vessels and cargoes left the Columbia River:

> H.B.Co. bark *Columbia*, 900 barrels of flour.
>
> American bark *Toulon*, 386 barrels of flour and 94,000 feet of lumber.
>
> American brig *Commodore Stockton*, 450 barrels of flour.
>
> American brig *Henry*, 70,000 feet of lumber and 96,000 shingles.

Allowing for loading, a vessel could make a round trip between Oregon and San Francisco in about two months, with a handsome profit on the cargo traded at each end of the voyage. It was easy to see why merchants and ship captains were numerous among the capitalists and entrepreneurs of the Willamette River townsites.

Pettygrove, after moving to California in 1849, was later active in establishing the townsite of Port Townsend on Puget Sound. He returned to Portland from time to time, and was back in July 1850, when he participated in a Fourth of July celebration. Dr. McLoughlin, born in Canada and for years a British subject, was also present at the festivities honoring the American "Revolution," or "Rebellion." Each of these pioneers was invited to propose a toast, and the wording of their toasts revealed something of their characters. This was Pettygrove's toast:

> TO OUR REVOLUTIONARY STRUGGLE — It won a home for freedom in the world, and the echoes of its warfare still rumble about the rotten monarchies of Europe.

It was a timely toast that showed Pettygrove as an inspired phrase-maker, a student of history, and a rather fiery "Liberal"—in the nineteenth-century meaning of that word.

For McLoughlin, the drink to the toast Pettygrove had proposed must have been a little hard to swallow, even though he had become a loyal American. His own toast was entirely non-political, with a more provincial patriotism:

> TO OREGON — From the fertility of its soil, the salubrity and mildness of its climate, the finest place in North America for the residence of civilized man.

Another occasion when Pettygrove returned to Portland was the reunion of the Oregon Pioneer Association, in 1880. By then he was 68, a spare, erect man of medium height, with a full white beard. A reporter from a Portland newspaper who interviewed Pettygrove at that time wrote: "It was his sagacity which saw at this site opportunities for commercial greatness and his enterprise which laid deep the foundation of that prosperity which is ours today." Pettygrove was quoted as saying, "I never sit down," which, the reporter observed, "reveals that spirit and energy which have given character and results to his busy life." Looking at the Portland of 1880, with its population of nearly 20,000, compared with the few hundred in 1848 when he sold out, Pettygrove said, "It fills my heart with joy to see this great city where I once saw dense woods."

8. GOLD HITS THE TOWNSITES

IF THE NEWS of the gold discovery in California could arouse an irresistible curiosity in a conservative and prudent Yankee trader like Pettygrove, it produced a veritable frenzy among the many more volatile settlers who had so recently demonstrated their venturesomeness by migrating across the plains. With an urgent lust for gold, they threw their packs on horses, or crowded onto small sailing vessels, for a general exodus to California.

The first report of the gold discovery reached Oregonians, like all the news they received in those days, in a delayed and circuitous way. The initial gold discovery, on the American River east of the town of Sacramento, had occurred in January 1848. On July 31, 1848, a small schooner, the *Honolulu*, Captain Newell, entered the Columbia, direct from San Francisco. This was surprising, because ordinarily she sailed only between San Francisco and Hawaii. The captain reported he had come in "for provisions." However, he proceeded up the river to Portland and began quietly buying up all the picks, shovels, and clothes the *Honolulu* could hold, paying for them in gold dust. Significantly, Captain Newell had neglected to bring any newspapers with him, an oversight noted by the editor of the *Spectator*. It was the custom of captains—editors felt it was their obligation—to pick up any newspapers they could find, before leaving a port, and to pass them along to the editor at their destination. Clippings from such papers were the chief source of all "news" that was not purely local—some issues of the *Spectator* were almost entirely "clips."

The newspapers of the 1840s and 1850s carried many little notices thanking "the gentlemanly Captain . . . for his courtesy in bringing the papers." But Captain Newell had carefully omitted to bring any. However, a few days after the *Honolulu* had reached Portland, a British naval vessel visited Fort Vancouver—Hudson's Bay Company still had a small but dwindling establishment there—and Captain Courtenay, of H.B.M.S. *Constance* brought some copies of an Hawaiian newspaper, the *Polynesian*. He promptly sent them up the river to the editor of the *Spectator*. In the *Polynesian* of June 24, 1848, the editor found an interesting item, which he reprinted in the *Spectator* of August 10th, and that was the first knowledge the people of Oregon had of a discovery which was to affect, in a dramatic way, the lives of almost every one of them. In printing the "clipping," the *Spectator* editor prefaced it by saying, "The following accounts for the appearance of the *Honolulu* in Oregon at this time."

CALIFORNIA

A terrible fever has nearly depopulated the California seaport towns and caused a general rush to the interior. It is not exactly the yellow fever, but a fever for a yellow substance called gold. An exceedingly rich gold mine has been discovered in the Sacramento Valley, and all classes and sexes have deserted their occupations and rushed *en masse* to the mines. The gold taken from this newly discovered mine is not gold ore, but pure virgin gold. It is procured by the simple process of digging and washing, at the rate of from two to four ounces per day by each laborer. It passes current at San Francisco for $15 per ounce.

The editorship of the *Spectator* was a part-time job, and the editor at this time was a lawyer, Aaron Wait,

practicing in Oregon City. With the judicious caution of
his profession, he recommended that Oregonians not
rush to the "diggings." He commented:

> If all our neighbors upon the Pacific will devote
> their time to gold digging, the citizens of Oregon
> will be able to obtain their share of the spoils by
> obtaining a remunerative price for their flour, peas,
> oats, potatoes, butter, cheese, fish, and lumber.

But few heeded the restraining words of the lawyer-
editor.

If the reprint from the *Polynesian* was not entirely
convincing, and the rumors surrounding the mysterious
visit of the *Honolulu* somewhat vague, all doubts vanished when, a few days after the publication of the news
in the *Spectator*, the brig *Henry* arrived. The *Henry* was
well-known on the river, being on a more or less regular run between Oregon and San Francisco, and her
captain, William K. Kilborn, was a respected merchant
at Oregon City, where he later (1850) was elected
mayor. He confirmed the gold discovery, not only ver-
bally, but by bringing the welcomed California newspapers, with all the details. The editor of the *Spectator*
acknowledged their receipt "through the politeness of
Captain Kilborn," and noted that there were no California papers after July 15th. The California newspapers
proved the magnitude of the gold discovery in a convincing way: they had had to suspend publication because all their printers had run off to the "diggings."
The *Spectator*, in its issue of August 24th, reported that
"Quite a number of our fellow citizens are leaving and
preparing to leave for the gold mine of the Sacramento."
Cautious as ever, however, the editor added, "We hope
they may find gold abundant and disappointments

scarce, but we fear the boot may come on the other leg."
By the next issue, September 7th, even the editor of the
Spectator had become a little emotional:

> GOLD MANIA!
> Oregon is convulsed by an excitement such as
> was never before felt here. What power gold has!
> Many excellent citizens are leaving, and preparing
> to leave—some by sea, some by land with horses,
> some with wagons. Keep cool, gentlemen, it will
> take years to dig it all out.

After that, there were no more issues of the *Spectator*
for more than a month. When it reappeared, October
12th, the editor wrote:

> ☞ The Spectator, after a temporary sickness,
> greets its patrons and hopes to serve them, as here-
> tofore, regularly. That "gold fever," which has swept
> 3000 of the officers, lawyers, physicians, farmers
> and mechanics from Oregon into the mines of Cali-
> fornia, took away our printers also.

The effect of all this on the townsites along the Willamette was dramatic. According to one report, by the
summer of 1849 there were only three men left at Portland: Lownsdale, a Colonel William King, and a Mr.
Warren. That report is difficult to corroborate, but even
allowing for exaggeration due to the genial desire to tell
a good story, it is clear, from many eyewitness accounts,
that few men remained at the townsites. Women and
children were left to clerk in the stores and to row their
boats into the towns to trade. According to one estimate,
by 1849 two-thirds of the Oregon population capable of
bearing arms had left for California. Construction at the
townsites almost ceased, due to the shortage of labor
and materials. An incidental result of the lack of manpower was noted in a letter written in April 1849 from a

minister reporting on the affairs of a new church at Oregon City:

"The church is unfinished and through the winter has been so very cold that it was impossible to keep it comfortable, so that at times the congregation has been very small. The Sabbath School was quite good during last summer, but the gold fever took away the teachers and the cold kept away the scholars, so that during the winter it has been the day of small things."

Though the "gold rush" temporarily drained manpower from Oregon, this depressive effect was soon more than offset by the stimulation of the Oregon economy through California's desperate demand for food and lumber. The demand for these things resulted not only from the immigration, as adventurers from all over the world converged on San Francisco, but also because many of the men already in California quit their regular occupations to dig for gold. The San Francisco waterfront looked like an extensive forest of bare trees—the masts of hundreds of vessels whose crews had abandoned them, to go for the gold. But it was a great day for those shipowners and captains who managed to keep their crews. For example, the brig *Sequin*, in the coastal trade between Oregon and San Francisco, on one round trip in 1849 made a net profit for her captain of $18,000, a very respectable sum in 1849 dollars. Early in 1849, lumber could be bought in Oregon for $30 per thousand board feet, and sold for $120 in San Francisco. Later in 1849, when the California boom was wildest and the shortages most acute, lumber was selling for $350 per thousand board feet, though cost of production in Oregon had also risen, to as much as $100 per thousand, due to the scarcity of labor. Trade in food products was also highly profitable. In 1849, a group of farmers along the lower Columbia River built a small schooner, hired a captain, and, with the farmers themselves as crew, took a cargo of produce to San Francisco, where it brought fantastic prices. Anyone who could get a crew together could buy a vessel cheaply, since there were so many of them abandoned in San Francisco and for sale. The cost of the vessel could be cleared on the first voyage, so that all subsequent trips netted great profit.

A vivid account of California's gold-boom economy and of the frantic demand for Oregon's lumber is given in a letter written by Benjamin Stark from San Francisco in June 1849. The letter was reproduced in the *Daily Chronicle*, of New London, Connecticut, in July 1849. The preface to the letter contains interesting biographical details about Stark, who was still owner of a half-interest in the Portland townsite. Stark, after buying that half-interest in the Portland claim from Lovejoy in November 1845, had continued as cargomaster on the *Toulon*, plying between Portland, Hawaii, and San Francisco, during 1845-47. In 1848, he had returned to his home in Connecticut. In the spring of 1849, drawn by the rumors from the gold fields, he returned by ship to San Francisco, arriving in June 1849. Following is the article from the *Daily Chronicle*:

> Letter from California—We make the following extract of a letter from Mr. Benjamin Stark, of this city, to his friend here. The letter is dated San Francisco, June 20, 1849, and was received here July 29th. Mr. Stark is a young man of great intelligence, shrewdness, and enterprise, and those who know him as we do will not only rely with confidence upon the facts he states, but give great weight to the opinions and inferences he may draw from them.
>
> "My Dear S - - -: I arrived here on the 4th inst. [June 1849], 46 days from New York, though trav-

elling but 28. The steamers are now to leave this
port regularly on the 1st of each month, so that the
journey may be made within a month. I find the
accounts received at home were but little if at all
exaggerated. Day laborers command $6 per day.
Servants are paid by those who can secure them
$250 per month. The scarcity of shelter for goods
compels much property of a perishable nature to
be sacrificed. Nearly one-half of the population is
living in tents, the scarcity of lumber preventing the
erection of buildings as rapidly as they are required.
The commonest lumber is selling at $350 [per thou-
sand board feet] just at this time. I have seen
Dr. Comstock. He says he can make more money
here in one month than he could in New London
in two years."

With this lucrative stimulus to trade, the number of
vessels coming to the Willamette increased greatly. Prior
to the "gold rush," during the nine-month period from
March to December 1847, there were nine arrivals in
the Willamette, or an average of about one per month.
By comparison, during the five months from May to
October 1849, an average of about five vessels per month
entered the Willamette. Once, during 1849, there were
20 vessels in the Willamette at one time, taking on cargo.

All of this trade brought substantial amounts of gold
into Oregon. As much as $1 million worth of gold dust
had been injected into the Oregon economy by the
spring of 1849, and much larger amounts came in thereafter. Many of the men who had gone to the mines
began returning during 1849, bringing back with them
gold dust and nuggets. By the fall of 1849, as many were
returning to Oregon from California as were leaving, and
Oregon's population growth resumed. With the continued demand for Oregon products in California, business

boomed. The gold brought into Oregon provided a much-needed lubricant for trade. Up to that time, there had been little gold or coin in Oregon. Instead, orders issued by merchants in exchange for furs, wheat, and other products circulated as "money." These orders allowed the bearer to present them at the issuing store for goods worth the face value of the order. The orders issued by these merchants, instead of being presented to the store for goods, might also change hands, in general circulation. Thus, there was "Hudson's Bay Money," "Abernethy Money," and "Pettygrove Money." In public circulation, however, these orders were only accepted if the persons offering them as "money" would discount the face value. The discounts varied widely and unpredictably, depending upon the desirability of the stock of goods in the particular merchant's store, for that was the only collateral backing such "money."

Another circulating medium in Oregon before the gold rush was the "script" issued by the Provisional Government to pay for its operations. This "script" was of dubious value and no one wanted to accept it in payment of a debt unless its face value was discounted. These various forms of "money," inadequate within Oregon, had no value whatsoever for purchases of manufactured goods outside Oregon. Trade between Oregon and Hawaii or "the States" was mostly on a barter basis, as were many transactions within Oregon.

Commodities, too, circulated as "money." For example, when the Provisional Government had matured to the point where it felt it could collect taxes, it had to take their payment in produce. The Revenue Act of 1846 included this provision:

"It is required of all those who pay their taxes in wheat that they bring and deliver the same at the following places: Clatsop County, Hudson's Bay Company's warehouse at Astoria; Vancouver County, Hudson's Bay Company's warehouses at Cowlitz or Fort Vancouver; Twality County, the county warehouse at Linnton or F. W. Pettygrove's warehouse at Portland; Klackamas County, the flour mill of John McLoughlin or the Milling Company at Oregon City; Champoick County, Hudson's Bay Company's warehouse at Champoick or the Milling Company's warehouse at the Bute; Yam Hill County, at such places as the collector for Yam Hill County shall direct."

The gold brought into Oregon beginning late in 1848 changed all this by providing a universally acceptable medium of exchange. The Oregonians coming back from the mines used their gold to pay off debts, improve their farms or businesses, and build houses. And, of course, those who had remained in Oregon, busy producing and shipping food and lumber, as the editor of the *Spectator* had advised, were paid in gold. The men who stayed quietly on their farms, raising food to ship to the miners and to the crowd of urban followers catering to the miners, reaped a richer harvest than many of those who developed callosities at the diggings.

9. AN ENERGETIC RIVAL AT MILWAUKIE

THE MOST ENERGETIC townsite promoter in taking advantage of the booming California market was Lot Whitcomb, the principal proprietor of Milwaukie. While the period from late 1848 until 1850 was one of exodus from most of the townsites, with building held back by lack of labor and materials, Milwaukie was a spectacular exception. The industrious Whitcomb and his associates worked so untiringly that the population at Milwaukie grew from nothing early in 1848 to about 500 by 1850. Portland's growth, meanwhile, had gone into a temporary slump, and its population was only about 300 in early 1850. This was the first serious challenge to the proprietors of the Portland townsite.

Whitcomb was the first to establish lumber shipments to San Francisco from the Willamette River. He did not agree with Captain Couch or the editor of the *Spectator* that the head of navigation was at Portland, and in 1848 he set out to prove that it was at Milwaukie. The *Spectator* reported in November 1848 that "Lot Whitcomb, Esq., our enterprising friend, and proprietor of the embryo city of Milwaukie" had commenced construction at Milwaukie of two small schooners to be used in the coasting trade between his town and California. Upon hearing the first news of the gold discovery, Whitcomb had quickly decided how Milwaukie could best take advantage of the opportunity. He had at once set about building vessels . . . "Quick decisions followed by quick action," as Napoleon had expressed the reason for his successes. Whitcomb also organized a crew to cut square timbers of the sort needed as supports in mines, paying the woodsmen enough to make it worth their while to resist the temptation to go to the gold fields. Here was an alert foe, indeed, to challenge the other townsites.

The editor of the *Spectator*, in enlarging upon Whitcomb's ship-building project, added some observations which help fill in the picture of Whitcomb's personality:

> The great and increasing demand for vessels upon the coast renders this enterprise one of general interest to the people of Oregon, and we trust that it

may prove as profitable as it is laudable for its pro-
jector. The present is not a propitious time for ship-
building, so far as laborers and materials aside from
timber and lumber are concerned; but unless friend
Whitcomb left his enterprise, forecast, and persever-
ance east of the mountains (and we don't think he
did), he will complete (life and death spared) all
that he commences.

Though some downstream rivals made light of the
idea that the head of navigation was as far upstream as
Milwaukie, there was no question about another essen-
tial ingredient for the successful growth of a town: the
energy and imagination of its proprietor. Whitcomb was
a vigorous, determined competitor of Portland. Lot
Whitcomb was born in 1806 in Vermont, another of
those New Englanders who were so important in early
Oregon's development. He married a Vermont girl and,
about 1830, migrated to Michigan. He became a con-
tractor and did work in Pennsylvania and in Illinois,
where he participated in the construction of a portion
of the canal connecting Chicago with the Mississippi
River. He was a member of the Illinois Legislature. In
the 1840s, he, like so many others, began to hear won-
derful reports about "Oregon."

Whitcomb decided the new frontier in Oregon would
be a great place for contractors and enterprising businessmen. In the spring of 1847, a party of 13 families,
including Whitcomb's, left Illinois together, bringing
with them enough money and equipment to make a
good beginning in a new country. Among the supplies
Whitcomb brought were the metal parts for a sawmill.
In Missouri, they joined other families, for a total of 114
wagons. Whitcomb was elected "Captain," a title that
stuck with him for the rest of his life. Whitcomb's fam-

ily at this time included his wife and three daughters. The youngest, who was just two years old, had been christened "Queen Victoria Whitcomb"—she was called "Queenie" for short! No record has been left to tell us what inspired the Whitcombs to name their daughter after the then young and beautiful Empress of Britain. It cannot be supposed, however, that it was done in levity; Lot Whitcomb was a very serious-minded man— proud, even dour—who was not given to jokes. Perhaps his or his wife's family, like some old New England colonists, had a loyalist tradition. Certainly, Whitcomb embodied many of those virtues we have come to call "Victorian."

Whitcomb reached Oregon City in November 1847, eight months after having left Illinois. When he arrived, he was ill, according to the *Spectator*, "from care, anxiety, and over-exertion for his company," and was some time recovering. The hotel register at Sidney Moss's "Main Street House" at Oregon City shows "Captain Whitcomb" as a guest late in 1847. Early in 1848, Whitcomb chose as his location the square mile where Johnson Creek enters the Willamette, a suitable site for the sawmill he planned to start. He named the townsite "Milwaukie," after the city in Wisconsin which he had seen and admired. The spelling of the last syllable was changed from "kee" to "kie," perhaps with a view to avoiding confusion in the nation when both had become great cities.

In the spring of 1848, Whitcomb was busy erecting a water-powered sawmill at the mouth of Johnson Creek. At the same time, he was acting as Commissary-General under the Provisional Government, an office to which he was named soon after his arrival in Oregon, indicating he was a man of impressive personality whose qualities were quickly recognized. One of his jobs as Commissary-General was to organize supplies for the regiment raised by the Provisional Government to suppress the Cayuse Indians, after their massacre of Dr. Whitman and other missionaries at Waiilatpu (near present-day Walla Walla).

Whitcomb's sawmill had just started running when, in August 1848, news of the gold discovery reached the Willamette. The timing, though fortuitous, could not have been better. While most men left for the mines, Whitcomb perceived that there would be a great demand for lumber, and he stayed at his mill. This mill sawed the boards for Clackamas County's first public school, at Milwaukie, and for the two schooners Whitcomb built and used to ship lumber to California. In 1848, Milwaukie also had "a good, commodious warehouse and two or three other buildings," and Whitcomb had established a free ferry across the Willamette. Whitcomb's sawmill became even more profitable when, during the winter of 1849-50, a flood washed away or damaged most of the other sawmills along the Willamette. Whitcomb, however, had built his mill above the flood level, so it was not affected. In 1849, Whitcomb built a flour mill at the mouth of Johnson Creek, near his sawmill. Flour was, like lumber, in great demand in California. The free ferry Whitcomb provided was primarily for the convenience of the Tualatin Valley farmers in bringing their grain to his mill. The editor of the *Spectator* was impressed by the maneuver, and wrote: "This spirit of enterprise, at a time when most minds are carried captive by the mania for gold digging, is worthy of commendation."

Milwaukie also had Oregon's first fruit tree nursery. It was established by Henderson Luelling, who crossed the plains in 1847, about the same time as the Whitcombs. Luelling came from a North Carolina family of nursery-men and orchardists. He moved from North Carolina to Indiana in 1831 and to Iowa in 1839. He was inspired to come to Oregon by reading the *Journals* of Lewis and Clark. In specially constructed wagons, he brought 700 grafted fruit trees, berry and grape vines, bushes, and peach pits. Accompanying Luelling and his wife were their eight children, who were very helpful in looking after the seedlings. The Luellings, with their four wag-ons, made most of the trip across the plains alone; they travelled slower than other immigrants because of fre-quent stops to water the plants. They reached the Willamette Valley late in November 1847, and spent the winter in an abandoned log cabin on the east bank of the Willamette opposite Portland. During the winter, Luelling looked for a good place for his nursery. He selected a claim adjacent to Whitcomb's. There, early in 1848, at the northern edge of present-day Milwaukie, he planted Oregon's first nursery. A few scattered fruit trees, gnarled hazards along the fairways of Waverley golf course, survive today, and remind inaccurate golfers of Luelling's nursery.

Another pioneer of 1847, Ralph C. Geer, recalling Luelling's nursery, said, many years later, "That load of trees contained health, wealth, and comfort for the old pioneers of Oregon. It was the mother of all our early nurseries and orchards, and gave Oregon a name and fame she would never have had without it."

Luelling, who was 38 years old when he arrived in Oregon, was an enterprising addition to Milwaukie.[3]

While waiting for his nursery stock to reach retail size, Luelling and some associates built a second sawmill on Johnson Creek in 1849, and in 1850, they added a flour mill. Thus, by 1850, Milwaukie had two sawmills, two flour mills, and a shipyard.

Milwaukie's shipyard was operated by Joseph Kellogg, who was from a Vermont family, later a resident of Ohio. He was 36 years old when he brought his family across the plains in the immigration of 1848. On reaching Oregon that fall, he took up a claim on the square mile just south of Milwaukie, and was immediately commissioned by Whitcomb to build a vessel capable of taking a cargo of lumber to California. Also active in the shipbuilding enterprise was Whitcomb's son-in-law, William Torrence. Torrence had married Whitcomb's oldest daughter (who bore the more conventional name, Mary Jane) in 1848, when she was 17 years old. Torrence held the claim on the square mile on the west side of the Willamette River opposite Milwaukie.

At Kellogg's shipyard, on the riverfront just south of Whitcomb's sawmill and flourmill, two small schooners were built. The first was christened the *Milwaukie*. She was a vessel of 22 tons, hardly more than a yacht. The *Milwaukie* was loaded with lumber from Whitcomb's sawmill and taken down the coast to San Francisco. There, she and her cargo were traded for a much larger vessel, the brig *Forrest*, 238 tons. The Milwaukie proprietors used the *Forrest* to ship lumber to California. Whitcomb's mill was producing 6000 board feet of lumber a day, in two 12-hour shifts. Most of this was in the form of rough, unplaned 3-inch planks. It sold at Whitcomb's mill for $100 per thousand feet, but at San Francisco for $300 per thousand.

With the profits from the lumber trade, Whitcomb and his associates acquired another vessel, the bark *Louisiana*, 299 tons. Subsequently, they added another and larger vessel to their line, the bark *Ocean Bird*, 415 tons. By 1851, they had added still another, the bark *Keoka*.

The editor of the *Spectator* was sufficiently impressed by developments at Milwaukie during 1848 and 1849 to revise the opinion he had expressed in April 1847 that the head of navigation was at Portland. Now, in the issue of December 13, 1849, he wrote:

> Milwaukie may be said to be the head of ship navigation on the Willamette. We are assured that any vessel that can come into the river at all can come up to Milwaukie.

The editor then went on to urge the merchants of Oregon City to use their influence with shippers to bring their cargoes to Milwaukie, for transfer to bateaus for the trip to Oregon City, rather than have the transfer made farther down the river, at Portland for example. Clearly, the editor was doing his best for Whitcomb, whom he liked to identify as "our enterprising friend, Lot Whitcomb, Esq."

Whitcomb was energetically pushing exports to California, and he was confident that Milwaukie had a great

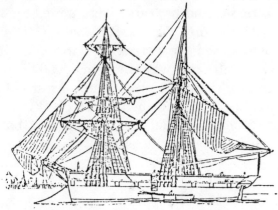

Brigantine

future. He placed this advertisement in the *Spectator* in January 1850, continuing it through the spring:

NOTICE TO SHIPOWNERS & MERCHANTS

THE undersigned, having been appointed agent for the disposal of lumber manufactured at Oregon City, Clackamas, and Milwaukie, the present head of navigation on the Willamette, will be ready at all times to contract for shipping or for sale by the cargo or retail, lumber, timber, shingles, etc.

He is also the agent for a line of ships running between San Francisco and this place. Vessels will be loaded with great dispatch, as the cargo can be taken from the shore or rafts.

LOT WHITCOMB
Milwaukie

In February 1850, a post office was established at Milwaukie, with Whitcomb as post master. It was the twelfth post office to be established in Oregon. Archrival Portland's post office had been established three months earlier, in November 1849, the third post office in Oregon.

Physically, the Milwaukie of 1850 was not imposing: houses and shacks of raw, unpainted lumber; dirt streets which were only muddy ruts during the winter; hogs and cattle roaming at large. However, in these respects, is was at no disadvantage relative to its rivals. Oregon City, it was true, presented a neater appearance, but, as we have seen, that city was an observer rather than a contender in the battle for metropolitan supremacy. And, by 1850, Milwaukie had, in addition to its four mills and shipyard, two hotels, a sheet iron and copper plating works, a public school, and about 500 inhabitants — a larger population than any other community in Oregon except Oregon City. The time had come for the rival proprietors downstream at Portland to take some action.

10. THE PORTLAND TRIO:
LOWNSDALE - COFFIN - CHAPMAN

AFTER SEPTEMBER 1848, when Pettygrove sold out his interest in the Portland townsite for a heap of leather, the destiny of "Little Stumptown" was, for about six months, in the hands of Lownsdale alone. Stark, the nominal owner of the other half-interest in the venture, had made occasional visits to Portland during 1845-47, aboard the *Toulon*, but, in 1848, had left the Pacific Coast to go back to his home in Connecticut. He returned to California in 1849 and visited Portland in the summer of 1850. Couch, who was later to be active in helping develop Portland, continued to live at Oregon City until late in 1847, when he made a voyage back to Massachusetts. He did not return to Oregon until August 1849. So, after Pettygrove's departure, it was up to Lownsdale to promote Portland's interests.

In order to bring in new capital and enterprise, Lownsdale, in March 1849, sold one-half of his half-interest in the Portland townsite to Stephen Coffin. Thus, Coffin and Lownsdale became equal partners, each owning a one-quarter interest. Coffin had come across the plains, with his wife and children, in the migration of 1847, settling at Oregon City. He was born in Maine. He had not come to Oregon as a wealthy man, but, after two years of hard work, at construction, contracting, and merchandising, he had accumulated considerable capital. He paid $6000 for the one-quarter interest in the Portland townsite. This was a nice gain for Lownsdale, who, just six months earlier, had paid Pettygrove only

$5000 for the entire half-interest. When Coffin bought half of Lownsdale's interest in Portland, he moved from Oregon City to Portland, and was energetic and resourceful in building up the town. Coffin was the prime mover in numerous enterprises of decisive importance in Portland's battle with her competitors.

The summer of 1849, after Coffin moved there, was still a quiet time at Portland as far as building was concerned, though there was great activity on the wharf, as vessels hurriedly loaded lumber and produce for California. Wishing still further to broaden the base of ownership and working capital, Lownsdale and Coffin, in December 1849, sold part of their interests to William W. Chapman, a lawyer at Oregon City. On January 1, 1850, Chapman, his family, and household goods were "bateaued" from Oregon City to Portland, and he had a house built where the County Courthouse now stands. Chapman, born in Virginia in 1808, had had extensive legislative experience in Iowa before he crossed the plains to Oregon in 1847. He was practicing law at Salem when he heard the call of the gold fields. He was at the mines from the fall of 1848 to the spring of 1849, and, being among the earliest prospectors, he was quite successful. On his return to Oregon, he had moved to Oregon City. However, it had become apparent to him that the metropolitan future did not lie there. A thorough exploration of the potentialities of the townsites along the lower Willamette convinced him that Portland was the site where transportation by land and ship could most readily meet. Lownsdale and Coffin each sold one-third of their interests to Chapman. The result of these dealings in fractions was that, as of December 1849, the

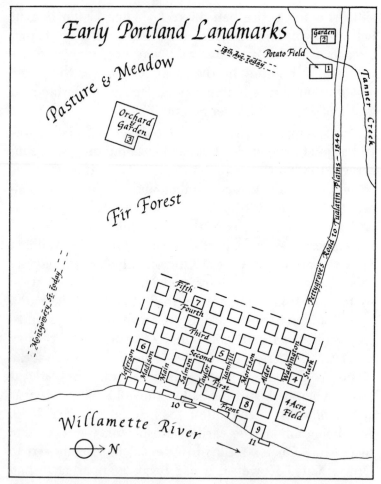

(1) Daniel Lownsdale's first house at Portland, built in 1845; (2) Houses built by Lownsdale in 1846 and 1847; (3) Lownsdale's residence beginning in 1854; (4) Residence of Stephen Coffin from August 1850 to February 1851; (5) Residence of Coffin from March 1851 to April 1852; (6) Residence of Coffin from May 1852 to May 1856; (7) Residence of William W. Chapman from 1850 to September 1853; (8) Original location of T. J. Dryer's weekly *Oregonian;* (9) Store and warehouse of Francis W. Pettygrove, Portland's first commercial enterprise; (10) Area used for moorage and loading of

(Continued on opposite page)

square mile within which lay the Portland townsite was distributed among these undivided interests:

Benjamin Stark, one-half interest

Daniel Lownsdale, one-sixth interest

Stephen Coffin, one-sixth interest

William Chapman, one-sixth interest

In January 1850, Lownsdale made a voyage to San Francisco, where he met Stark. The two agreed to simplify the ownership of the square mile containing the Portland townsite, in order to avoid future controversy and to make it easier to sell lots. It had been cumbersome to convey title to newcomers under the joint and complex ownership. Lownsdale and Stark agreed that all land north of Stark Street would belong solely to Stark, the remainder of the square mile being held jointly by Lownsdale, Coffin, and Chapman. Since most of the lots in Stark's portion had already been sold, it was further agreed that the other three owners would pay Stark the amount they had received for those lots. Stark's portion was bounded by the river, Stark Street, and the northern edge of the original claim—about Burnside Street—where it joined Couch's claim.

It might seem that Stark's small, wedge-shaped area was an inadequate representation of a "half interest." His portion contained only 48 acres, while the other three as a group got almost 600 acres. However, Stark's area, though small, contained many of the businesses and buildings in the Portland of 1850. The other three owners, for the

sailing vessels along the riverbank where the Willamette River closely approached Front Street; (11) Portland's first wharf, built for Pettygrove by John Waymire. (Based upon a map drawn by Lownsdale, a copy of which is in the possession of the Pioneer National Title Insurance Co., in Portland.)

half their combined interests represented, got fewer buildings but a much larger area for potential future growth. Actually, Stark did extremely well, considering that he had paid Lovejoy only about $390 for the half-interest in 1845, had taken no active part in developing the townsite, and indeed had not set foot in it since 1847. After visiting Portland in the summer of 1850, Stark returned to San Francisco, to engage in shipping, merchandising, and banking. Later, though after Portland's victory over her rivals had been established, he came to live at Portland. From October 1861 to September 1862, he was U.S. Senator, appointed by the Governor to fill a vacancy. Politically, Stark was a Southern Democrat. Though he was educated in Connecticut and later made his home there, he had been born in New Orleans.

Lownsdale-Coffin-Chapman were an effective and well-balanced team. They possessed large amounts of capital, for that time and place, and rapidly accumulated more from sale of lots to men returning from the mines and to new immigrants. They brought together a wide experience in business, law, construction, and merchandising. Lownsdale and Chapman were Southern Democrats, and Coffin was in the New England Whig tradition, later becoming a leading Oregon Republican. But mutual self-interest in the Portland townsite over-rode, for the time, any friction these political differences might have caused. Of the three, none was as uniquely important as Pettygrove had been to the period 1845-48. Chapman only remained at Portland till 1853. In that year, he bought Fort Umpqua from Hudson's Bay Co., with the intention of using it as a center for a cattle business, and moved with his family to southern Oregon. He retained his investment in the Portland townsite, however. After several years of various ventures, moves, and jobs, he returned to live at Portland in 1861, but by then the battle of the townsites had long been decided. Coffin remained at Portland, and showed an energy and imagination in promoting Portland's interests that fully justified Lownsdale's judgment in bringing him in as a partner. Coffin was a leader in all the ventures and maneuvers that enabled Portland to overcome her rivals.

With Whitcomb pushing Milwaukie to the fore, Coffin brought in a new technology, steam, to meet that challenge. The *Spectator* in December 1849 reported that "a steam sawmill will soon be in operation at Portland." Coffin, after joining Lownsdale at Portland, made a trip to San Francisco in the summer of 1849 to find someone to help put up a steam sawmill. While Milwaukie's waterpower resource was not great, it was better than anything Portland had, and Milwaukie was making great profits with its water-powered lumber and flour mills. In San Francisco, Coffin met a millwright, William P. Abrams, and persuaded him to come to Portland. Abrams, who was 29 years old, was from New Hampshire and had his family with him. Coffin also found another recruit from New Hampshire, a young man named Cyrus Reed who, working in the booming San Francisco environment as a sign painter, had done very well financially. Abrams and Reed came to Portland in November 1849 aboard the brig *Sequin*. The steam sawmill was slowly put together and began operating in 1850. The first issue of the *Oregonian*, in December 1850, announced that, at Portland, "We have a steam sawmill already in operation and another about being erected."

The first steam sawmill at Portland, which was also the first one on the Pacific Coast, was put up by Abrams and Reed with the financial backing of Coffin, and had a capacity of 6000 feet of lumber a day. It was a very small operation by today's standards, about equal in capacity to Whitcomb's water-powered mill. Portland's steam sawmill was known as the "Abrams and Reed" mill, though Coffin, as a partner, provided capital and made it his business to market and ship the lumber. The timber for the Abrams & Reed mill was readily at hand: trees along what are now 2nd and 3rd Avenues. They were hauled only a few blocks to the mill, using a wagon with large wheels to enable it to roll over the ruts and deep holes in the unpaved streets.

The "old sawmill," as it was known for many years to early Portlanders, had the first industrial whistle ever to pierce the air of Oregon. The mill was located at the foot of Jefferson Street, where there has been continuously since then a sawmill in operation. In 1850, when the mill started up, there was an Indian settlement just to the south of the mill, in a flat area which today, given over to industry, has become a treeless tangle of tanks, towers and metallic shapes where no Indian would feel at home. When the Indians heard that the white man's new big tool was about to start working, they hesitatingly gathered round. Suddenly, the steam whistle shrieked; the Indians ran into the tall timber, then only a few steps away. There they remained for some time while the mill, hissing with jets of steam, slowly turned a log into rough planks. Portland's second steam sawmill, completed in 1851, had a capacity of 10,000 feet of lumber a day. Also, in that year, there was erected at Portland a steam flour mill. Thus, by 1851, Portland had an industrial base, built on steam, which at least equalled Milwaukie's.

With this industrial development under the leadership of the Portland Trio, Portland's population resumed growing in 1850, after the temporary slump of 1848-49. A revealing description of Portland at this time is given in a letter written by the wife of a sea captain who was at Portland from December 1849 to January 1850. A captain often made his sailing vessel almost a home, keeping his wife and family aboard. The wife of Captain Z. C. Norton, of the brig *Sequin*, wrote a letter, reproduced in the Oregon Historical Society *Quarterly*, which contained these observations:

"We dropped anchor off the little town of Portland. This place is yet in its infancy. Many of its inhabitants are Eastern people, engaged in commerce and presentable business. Lumber is abundant and those engaged in this trade are receiving great gain. A few fine buildings have been erected, and it already has the appearance of a pleasant little village. Yet you find here and there a log or stump to retard your progress. The principal owner of this little town [she was probably referring to Lownsdale, though Coffin was an equal co-owner at that time] who a few months ago was not worth a dollar is now said to possess $50,000. We are remaining in this place sufficient time to load with flour and timber, during which time I enjoyed myself well, and for the first time since I left my home [New England] have found the society and customs correspond with those of our own happy land. In this little town the Sabbath is more regarded than in any country I have found while rounding the mighty continent."

Mrs. Norton's comment about "stumps" was just one more reference, of many, to the feature that gave Portland its nickname. Eventually, some of the stumps were whitewashed, so people would not run into them in the dark. But despite its quaint idiosyncrasy, Portland was growing. At one time, during 1850, about 150 new houses were under construction at one time in "Little Stumptown." Another evidence of progress was the public spirit which prompted the residents of Portland to raise $700 for the relief of immigrants stranded above The Dalles in the fall of 1850. Many of those immigrants decided, perhaps as a result, to settle at Portland. By the end of 1850, Portland's population, which had temporarily been eclipsed by that of Milwaukie, had surged forward to at least equal that of her upstream rival.

11. A NEW WEAPON: THE PRINTING PRESS

LOT WHITCOMB AND HIS associates at Milwaukie had preceded Portland down the road toward industrialization, and had been first to tap the rich California market. The Portland Trio had overcome that initial advantage, with steam, and increased the tempo of competition. Now, the contestants shifted their ground, from manufacturing and trade to communications and culture. Any village with pretensions to becoming a great metropolis, the townsite promoters decided, must have a newspaper. Yet merchants and businessmen at both Milwaukie and Portland were obliged to place their advertisements in the Oregon City *Spectator*, the only newspaper in the whole Territory. A newspaper, properly edited, could do much to advance the interests of a townsite. Almost simultaneously, the rivals at Milwaukie and Portland took steps to remedy their deficiency. In the summer of 1850, Whitcomb, and

Coffin and Chapman, were all in San Francisco. Among other items on their shopping lists, they were looking for editors and printers. Again, Whitcomb beat his downstream rivals to the punch. His paper, the *Western Star*, made its appearance two weeks before Portland's *Oregonian*.

In San Francisco, Whitcomb found two young men who had been trained as printers, and who also, like Whitcomb, happened to be from Vermont. One was John Orvis Waterman, aged 24; the other was William Davis Carter, aged 22. Whitcomb immediately hired them to come to Milwaukie. They came up from San Francisco in August 1850 on the bark *Louisiana*, one of the vessels in Whitcomb's "Milwaukie Line." When word of the arrival of the printers at Milwaukie reached Oregon City, the publisher of the *Spectator* found it expedient, that very month, to increase the frequency of his publication from once every two weeks to once a week, demonstrating the benign influence of competition. The *Spectator* became a weekly with its issue of August 29, 1850.

The *Spectator*, in its issue of November 7, 1850 published this item:

> Milwaukie — The types, press, and materials for the printing of a newspaper have recently arrived at that place. We have not learned the name of the paper nor when it will make its appearance.

The materials and equipment for printing Milwaukie's newspaper arrived aboard the bark *Desdemona*, which entered the Columbia River October 19th. She came direct from New York and also brought merchandise for Abernethy & Co., of Oregon City. Because of the time required for communication and shipment, it is clear that Whitcomb had sent the order for the printing materials to New York early in 1850, months before he had found Waterman and Carter in San Francisco. Again, Whitcomb had shown the astute planning and forehandedness that made him a formidable rival.

The first issue of the new paper, named the *Western Star*, appeared November 21, 1850. It showed Lot Whitcomb as "Publisher," J. O. Waterman as "Editor," and "Waterman and Carter, Printers." The *Spectator* commented, somewhat condescendingly:

> The *Western Star* is the title of a new paper, the first number of which is now before us, just started at Milwaukie by Lot Whitcomb, Esq. The paper is well gotten up and presents rather a pretty face in its new suit. The paper comes out flatfooted Democratic.

The political color of the new paper was something of a surprise. It might have been expected that the two young newspapermen, coming from Vermont, would be Whigs. Whitcomb himself was, at this time, a Whig, though he was not rigidly partisan in politics. Up to this time, national party allegiance had not been a journalistic concern in Oregon. The only newspaper, the *Spectator*, gave its space to problems peculiar to Oregon. Its editor, D. J. Schnebly, who replaced lawyer Wait in the editorial chair in February 1849, was Whig in sympathy, but he tried to keep his paper free from party label. The majority of Oregonians at this time were Democrats, though the town population (at Oregon City, Milwaukie, and Portland) were predominantly Whig. While national party names had less significance out on the frontier than they had had back in the States from which the immigrants had come, the declaration by Editor

Waterman that the *Western Star* would be "Democratic" was welcomed by many potential subscribers. Perhaps Whitcomb was not annoyed to find that his young editor embraced the majority view. In fact, a few years later, Whitcomb himself had become a Democrat. Now, with Waterman stating bluntly, "In politics we are Democratic," Schnebly found himself gradually giving the *Spectator* an increasingly Whig line.

The *Western Star* office also did commercial printing, and could thus compete with the *Spectator* for such work as that needed by the Territorial Government. An incident in this connection illuminates the ruggedly individualistic character of our Milwaukie hero. In December 1850, a printing job had been offered by the Legislature to the *Western Star*. It was only a small job, with more nuisance value than profitability, and, when Whitcomb discovered just how small it was, he declined the contract, which was then given to the *Spectator*. Editor Schnebly, of the *Spectator*, in reporting these circumstances, stated that Whitcomb had "backed out" on the job. It was an unhappy choice of words. The phrase did not please our proud proprietor, who paid Schnebly a visit and required him to publish a retraction. So, in the following issue of the *Spectator*, Schnebly wrote.

> Mr. Whitcomb wishes us to state that we have falsified the facts connected with the letting of the public printing. We stated that the printing had been awarded to Mr. Whitcomb, but that, after ascertaining the amount to be executed, he was unwilling to take the contract—"he backed out." He wishes us to state that Lot Whitcomb *never* backs out. We shall leave it to him to make the distinction.

It was one small discord, attributable perhaps to the strains and frustrations under which they were working on the frontier, in an otherwise cordial friendship. The wording of the retraction must have offended Whitcomb's sensibilities again. But here he decided to let the matter drop, at least as far as the public record is concerned.

Meanwhile, down the river at rival Portland, the editor and publisher of that townsite's heralded newspaper was impatiently awaiting the arrival of his equipment. Coffin and Chapman, in San Francisco, had found their man in the person of Thomas Jefferson Dryer, whom they met, appropriately, on the Fourth of July. Dryer, from New York State, had come to California in 1849. He had had journalistic experience in both New York and California, and, 42 years old when the Portlanders met him, was a more mature editor than his young rivals at Milwaukie. When Coffin and Chapman met him, Dryer had an old hand press and some rather battered type and was looking for a promising place to start a newspaper. The Portland proprietors recruited him for their townsite. It was Chapman who suggested the eminently suitable name for the paper: the *Oregonian*.

Coffin and Chapman were back in Portland early in August and announced, with satisfaction, that Portland would soon have its own paper. The *Spectator* reported that "A Whig journal, the *Oregonian*, is to be published at Portland by T. J. Dryer," who, according to Coffin and Chapman, was a powerful orator and "a pungent writer."

Dryer arrived in Portland about the first of November 1850. The Portland proprietors provided a log shack, on

Morrison Street between Front and First, for his office and press. While waiting for his equipment, which had been shipped on a slower sailing vessel, Dryer toured the townsites along the Lower Willamette. The *Spectator*, early in November, printed this little profile:

> ☞ MR. DRYER, the editor and proprietor of the *Oregonian* that is to be, called to see us one day last week. He informed us that his press and materials were in the river, on their way to Portland. He expected to be able to issue the first number in about two weeks from that time. Mr. Dryer has been connected with the *California Courier* since its establishment, about a year since, and has displayed ability as editor through its columns. We were pleased with his first appearance. He looks as sharp as a steel trap.

If Dryer had had more luck with shipping, he might have been able to get out his first issue ahead of Whitcomb's *Western Star*. He had sent up his equipment on the bark *Keoka*, which left San Francisco October 8th. But the *Keoka* had been buffeted by headwinds and did not enter the Columbia River till November 9th. When Dryer, in the first week of November, had told editor Schnebly of the *Spectator* that his materials were "in the river," he knew that they certainly ought to be, according to the delivery date he had been promised in San Francisco. After its delayed arrival in the Columbia, the *Keoka's* trip up the river was also unusually slow. When the first issue of the *Western Star* came out, November 21st, the *Oregonian's* materials were still somewhere "in the river near Portland."

Editor Dryer, when he finally got out his first issue, December 4th, wrote an amusing and informative explanation for the delay in its publication:

Justice to ourselves, as well as to our readers, requires at our hands some explanation for the late appearance of the *Oregonian*. The facts are these: We shipped our materials and hands on the bark *Keoka*, at San Francisco, on the 8th of October, with the assurance from the agents there, and Capt. Hall, that she would be in the Columbia River in 12 days, at farthest. Upon our arrival here, we found the vessel had not yet arrived, although much more time had elapsed than was represented to us as requisite for the passage. After waiting nearly two weeks, we heard that the *Keoka* was in the river, and was hourly expected. Some week or more after the *Keoka* was reported as having left Astoria, and when forebearance had ceased to be a virtue almost, for us, Capt. Hall of the *Ocean Bird*, the father of the Capt. Hall of the *Keoka*, and one of the owners, who had just come up the river, was pointed out to us in the street. We approached him with as gentlemanly demeanor as we were capable of using, enquired of him when we might expect the *Keoka* to arrive, at the same time telling him we had some freight on board of her and that we were extremely anxious to receive it. He very bluntly and with apparent indignity told us he didn't know, neither did he care, and said, "We don't agree to deliver freight at any particular time." He abruptly left us, remarking that the amount of our freight was of little consequence to him.

In reply to an enquiry made afterwards by a gentleman who heard the conversation, as to who we were and what was the freight in question, Capt. Hall said, "He's a fellow who has come out here to print a little d - - n Whig paper in Portland."

Another week elapsed, and we were compelled to charter the "Skookum Chuck," Capt. James Coburn, with whom we took passage in search of the *Keoka*, which we found quietly reposing at her anchor some 50 miles below. After receiving the small amount of freight, which was of so little consequence to Capt. Hall of the *Ocean Bird*, but of con-

siderable to us, we commenced ascending the river.
Capt. Coburn accomplished the trip of 100 miles
in 2½ days, not with steam, but with the power of
six Indians.

Shortly after editor Dryer had removed his printing
equipment from the *Keoka*, she got under way and eventually arrived at Portland, 48 days after leaving San
Francisco. It is a curious coincidence that the Capt. Hall,
who was so disdainful about the arrival of Portland's
printing press, was closely associated with the Milwaukie townsite interests. Both his *Ocean Bird* and his
son's *Keoka* were part of Whitcomb's "Milwaukie Line"
of sailing vessels. Historians must take care not to read
into events explanations, however intriguing, which cannot be documented. But it would have been to Milwaukie's advantage to delay and inconvenience Portland's
new publication. Did the Captains Hall decide deliber-
ately to lay over, down the river, till the *Western Star*
could get one-up on Portland? No clear answer can be
given. However, the records do show that the *Ocean
Bird* and the *Keoka* both entered the Columbia November 9th, but that the *Keoka* reached Portland almost two
weeks after the *Ocean Bird*, though, presumably, they
experienced the same winds.

If the "Democratic" complexion of the *Western Star*
was unexpected, so also the "Whig" loyalty of Portland's
paper might have come as a surprise. Two members of
the Portland Trio — Lownsdale and Chapman — were
Southern Democrats. Chapman was later an office holder
under President Buchanan's Democratic administration.
He was appointed Surveyor General for Oregon in 1857
and held the office until 1861. He then resigned, declin-
ing to serve under President Lincoln, whose election he

had opposed. Coffin, on the other hand, was a Whig, later making the transition along with most other Whigs to the Republican Party, of which he became an active leader. This is one more piece of circumstantial evidence suggesting that Coffin was the dominant personality in the Portland Trio. His energy and imagination had already been revealed in previous enterprises, and would be shown further during the next few years.

The first issue of the *Oregonian* was greeted with approval by editor Schnebly of the *Spectator*:

> "The Oregonian" is the title of a new paper recently started at Portland, T. J. Dryer editor and publisher. The paper looks well, and the first number comes out as pleasant and smiling as a May morning. The *Oregonian* is to advocate the Whig side in politics. We congratulate the citizens of Portland upon their securing the services of so talented and energetic a man as Mr. Dryer to represent the interests of that portion of the Territory. Success to the editor, success to the *Oregonian*.

Schnebly, a Whig himself, felt more at home with the *Oregonian* than he did with Waterman's *Western Star*, but he tried to remain an independent force between the two. The three editors developed a gruff bonhommie in dealing with each other, calling one another "Brother," but the insults they hurled back and forth made it no game for a sensitive, thin-skinned soul.

A fourth newspaper, which began publication at Oregon City on March 25, 1851, should also be mentioned, but only in passing, as it had no connection with townsite rivalry on the Lower Willamette. This was the *Statesman*, begun as a personal political organ to advance the interests of the Democrat Party and especially the interests of Samuel Thurston, Territorial delegate to

Congress, who primarily arranged for the newspaper undertaking. The *Statesman* moved from Oregon City to Salem in June 1853, at the time the Oregon capital made the same move. The move of the capital was engineered by the Democrat majority in the Legislature, and the *Statesman* was the organ for the Democrats who controlled Oregon politics at that time.

With weekly newspapers at both townsites, Milwaukie and Portland seemed still to be on a more or less equal footing. Whitcomb's brief lead in newspaper publication had been matched by the Portland Trio, just as he had been at least matched, if not outdone, in manufacturing. Now, in 1850, there remained a key issue to be settled on another battlefield: shipping.

12. THE FIRST STEAMSHIPS: AN ADVANTAGE FOR PORTLAND

See note, page 169

BY 1850, SEVERAL VESSELS were carrying lumber and produce between Milwaukie and California. Of course, many vessels were also coming to Portland, as well as to points down the river. But Portland's promoters were looking for a way to establish unequivocal leadership over its rivals in shipping. Again, as they had with the sawmill, they found the answer in steam, and again it was Coffin who took the lead in the venture. The *Spectator*, in April 1850, printed this clipping from the *New York Herald*:

A NEW STEAMER TO PLY
BETWEEN OREGON
AND SAN FRANCISCO

Messrs. F. and D. Fowler and Captain C. A. Randlett, of New York City, and Stephen Coffin and H. H. Hunt of Oregon, have now in course of construction a steamer of 770 tons, to ply between Oregon and San Francisco. The vessel is in the yard of Westervelt and McKay and is of beautiful model. She is 193 feet long. When fully laden, she will draw but 9 feet of water, and will accomodate 200 passengers.

In June 1850, the *Spectator* printed a follow-up on construction of the steamship, which had been named the *Columbia*:[4]

The steamer *Columbia*, now being built in New York by Coffin & Co., of Portland, is expected to commence her regular trips in October or November, between Portland and San Francisco.

As it turned out, the *Columbia* did not reach the Pacific Coast until March 1851. When she did arrive, she was controlled by the Pacific Mail Steamship Company. Coffin had sold out his share in the *Columbia* to commit his capital to another steamship for Portland, the *Gold Hunter*. However, Coffin's early interest had stimulated construction of this vessel designed specifically for entering and navigating the Columbia and Willamette Rivers. The *Columbia* was described as "a sturdy little sidewheeler built especially for the coastal trade." Like all early steamships, she had sails to supplement steam.

Months before the *Columbia* reached Portland, however, the age of the steamship had already arrived. In June 1850, the *Spectator* printed a memorable announcement:

> The mail steamer, *Carolina*, arrived at Portland the 31st of May, six days from San Francisco. We hail this as a new era in the history of this Territory.

The *Carolina* was the first of the fleet of steamships sent out by the Pacific Mail Steamship Co., which had been given a contract and subsidy by the U.S. government to carry the mail up the Pacific Coast from Panama. The *Carolina* was a small vessel, only 149 feet long, of 544 tons. However, she required 14 feet of water. She had a propeller, rather than the side paddle-wheels used on many early steamships.

A few weeks after the first visit of the *Carolina*, an even more impressive vessel came to Portland—the U.S. Navy Steamship *Massachusetts*. On board were officials surveying Pacific Coast ports to establish lighthouses. She came into the Columbia River June 30, 1850 and arrived at Portland July 8th. The *Massachusetts*, which also had that innovation, a propeller, drew 17 feet of water, so that her safe arrival seemed to be a fairly convincing testimonial to Portland's accessibility for ocean shipping. The *Carolina* was again at Portland on June 25th and July 15th.

However, both the *Carolina* and the *Massachusetts* had made their trips to Portland during the period of annual high water. On the *Carolina's* next trip, early in August, the river level had fallen, and her captain thought it prudent not to come into the Willamette at all. Instead, he disembarked the passengers and mail at Fort Vancouver.

After its August trip, the *Carolina* was transferred to the increasingly busy run between Panama and San Francisco. The P.M.S.Co's. newer, larger vessels began to arrive on the Pacific Coast. They included the *California*, the *Panama*, and the *Oregon*. These were vessels of about 1000 tons, almost twice as large as the *Carolina*, though still precariously small by modern standards. They did not venture up the Columbia River at all. They came only to Astoria, stopping just long enough to discharge mail, passengers, and freight. Then they headed quickly back to San Francisco, to make a trip or two to Panama before their next hurried visit to Astoria. From Astoria, the mail was brought up the river by a small steamboat which had been built at Astoria by James Frost. It began running in July 1850, and could carry 20 passengers. The new P.M.S.Co. steamships made about five irregular and unpredictable mail deliveries to Astoria from September 1850 to the following March, when the *Columbia*, the ship Coffin had helped construct, arrived to provide a more or less regular service between San Francisco and the Columbia River.

There were more steamship glories for Portland in 1850, however. That June, the *Spectator* had reported:

> The steamer *Gold Hunter*, we learn, is to commence running in a short time between San Francisco and the Columbia.

That announcement was somewhat premature, as the *Gold Hunter* did not make her first appearance at Portland for six months. Before that, another little steamship had visited Portland, adding more momentum to the reputation Portland was gaining as a terminus for shipping. This new arrival was the *Sea Gull*, which reached Portland, after a seven-day passage from San Francisco, on September 30, 1850. A very small vessel of only 266 tons — hardly larger than a modern-day tugboat — she came up to Portland and went down the river without difficulty, clearing out over the Columbia River bar for San Francisco on October 6th. She was back at Portland again in January and again in February 1851.

The *Gold Hunter* finally did arrive at Portland December 1, 1850, six months after her visit had been forecast in the *Spectator*. The *Oregonian* of December 4, 1850, the first issue of that newspaper, contained this item:

> ☞ The steamer *Gold Hunter* took all by surprise on Sunday last [December 1st] by its unexpected arrival in our port. The *Gold Hunter* is one of the finest steamers on the Pacific, and commanded by an able, efficient, and gentlemanly officer. The *Gold Hunter* will sail in a day or two for San Francisco direct. A ball is to be given to the officers of the steamer this evening at the City Hotel.

The *Gold Hunter's* visit was in response to the efforts of the proprietors of the Portland townsite. They had been in San Francisco earlier in 1850, where they had used every occasion they could find to interest captains and shipowners in bringing a steamship to Portland. They minimized any difficulties in the river channel, and offered assurances that Portland could regularly provide full cargoes, which could easily be loaded at a wharf, for quick profits in California.

The ownership of the *Gold Hunter* was divided among numerous shareholders, and when she arrived, Portlanders were offered an entrancing proposition: ownership of the vessel. Enough of the owners were willing to sell out to give the Portlanders control. The total price for the majority interest was $60,000. The *Oregonian* reported:

> We have a prospect of securing the *Gold Hunter* as a regular Packet, to run between Portland and San Francisco. There is, perhaps, no steamer on the Pacific better adapted to this trade than the *Gold Hunter*. She combines speed, strength, safety, and comfort.

The *Gold Hunter* was, in comparison with ships seen on the river today, very small. She was 172 feet long, slightly longer than the *Carolina*, but of only 510 tons, compared to the *Carolina's* 544 tons. However, she had the advantage that she required less water than the *Carolina*, since she was designed to be propelled by side paddle-wheels rather than a propeller. The *Gold Hunter* was nearly twice the size of the *Sea Gull*.

It was dramatic evidence of the ample capital available to the Portland townsite proprietors that they were able, on short notice, to raise $21,000 in gold and currency, a very impressive sum in 1850. The sale of lots had been going along profitably, and the Portland Trio also had funds from their various other enterprises: importing and exporting, and manufacturing. Lawyer Chapman quickly organized a joint stock company, to buy up the majority interest in the steamer. Nearly all of the $21,000 cash was put up by Lownsdale, Coffin, and Chapman, with Coffin taking the largest share. Two other men purchased small shares. The remaining $39,000 was accepted by the sellers in the form of a personal note signed jointly by Lownsdale, Coffin, and Chapman.

Top Left: Hall Kelley, a Boston teacher who promoted Oregon settlement and planned a city on the Willamette in 1831.

Top Right: Nathaniel Wyeth, a Boston businessman who built a trading post (Fort William) on Sauvie Island in 1834.

Bottom: The *Lausanne*, drawn by H. Campbell, a passenger on its 1840 voyage to Oregon bringing Methodist missionaries.

Top: Oregon City as seen from the west bank of the Willamette at Linn City in 1845, painted by Henry Warre.

Bottom: The *Maryland,* drawn by Captain Couch in his log of the vessel's trip from New England to Oregon. He took the 90-foot brig up the Willamette to Oregon City in 1840.

Top: Sailing scows on the Columbia River. Transportation in Oregon in the 1850s was mostly by water.

Bottom Left: Hugh Burns came to Oregon in 1842 and founded the townsite of "Multnomah City," now part of West Linn.

Bottom Right: Rev. Alvin Waller arrived aboard the *Lausanne* in 1840 and opened a mission and store at Oregon City.

hum *servant* *for* *is* *sick* *and* *cant find* *his pants*
cook in darbys *middle part the wind*
veering & hauling *six points as much as we*
can do to keep *the sails trimed*

Top: The *Chenamus,* in which Captain Couch made his second voyage to Oregon, in 1842, sketched by Couch in his log.

Bottom: The U. S. Naval survey schooner *Shark,* under the direction of Lt. Neil Howison, who visited Oregon townsites in 1846.

Top: The 90-foot *Columbia,* first steamboat to run on the Willamette, began service in July 1850.

Bottom: The 160-foot *Lot Whitcomb,* launched at Milwaukie Christmas Day 1850, pride of the river for several years.

OPPOSITE PAGE:

Top: The riverboat *Lot Whitcomb* at Oregon City about 1852, with Linn City across the river in the distance.

Lower Left: Jacob Kamm, who helped build the *Lot Whitcomb* and was her first engineer.

Lower Right: John Ainsworth, captain of the *Lot Whitcomb.* In later years, when this photo was taken, he became a shipping financier and banker.

Top: Lot Whitcomb crossed the plains to Oregon in 1847 and became the principal promoter of the Milwaukie townsite.

Bottom Left: William Carter, printer of the weekly *Western Star,* published at Milwaukie 1850-51.

Bottom Right: Henderson Luelling brought Oregon's first fruit trees in 1847 and helped develop Milwaukie.

Top: Milwaukie, seen from the river's west bank, in 1851.

Bottom: Milwaukie in the late 1850s, seen from the ferry landing on the west bank of the Willamette.

Note: All the photographs and drawings in this picture section are reproduced through the courtesy of the Oregon Historical Society.

Top: An early flour mill and Milwaukie's main street, along the riverfront in the 1850s.
Bottom: The hotel at Milwaukie, an imposing structure in the 1850s.

Top: Francis W. Pettygrove, the Portland townsite's first developer, with his family, photographed in the 1870s.

Bottom Left: First structure on the Portland townsite, built in winter of 1844-45 at Front and Washington streets.

Bottom Right: Asa L. Lovejoy, immigrant of 1842 and lawyer at Oregon City, one of the Portland townsite's first owners.

Top Left: Daniel H. Lownsdale, a tanner, who bought Pettygrove's Portland claim in 1848 for $5000 worth of leather.

Top Right: William W. Chapman, a lawyer, who became a partner in developing the Portland townsite in December 1849.

Bottom Left: Zachariah Norton, captain of the brig *Sequin*, who settled in Portland in November 1850 and built a wharf.

Bottom Right: John Waymire, who built Portland's first wharf, in 1846, at the foot of Washington Street.

Top Left: Thomas J. Dryer, founder and editor of Portland's *Oregonian,* published his first issue December 4, 1850.

Top Right: Stephen Coffin was one of Portland's principal developers and a general in the Oregon militia of the 1860s.

Bottom Left: Capt. John Couch decided the head of navigation was at Portland and became a merchant and landowner there.

Bottom Right: Benjamin Stark bought an interest in the Portland claim in 1845, was U. S. Senator from Oregon, 1861-62.

Top: First Street, Portland, looking north from Oak Street, about 1851. At left: City Hall; at right, Molthrop's Hotel.

Right: Nathaniel Crosby came to Portland in 1845 as captain of the *Toulon,* in 1850 developed Milton as a rival townsite.

Bottom: Capt. Crosby's house, brought in sections from New England and erected at Portland by John Morrison in 1847.

Top: Portland's Front Street in 1852, looking south from Alder Street, with the brig *Henry* tied up along the riverbank.

Bottom: Portland's Front Street in the 1850s, looking south from Morrison Street. Center, a foundry; at left, Union Hotel.

Top: Portland's Front Street in 1852, looking south from Oak Street, showing civic leaders in top hats, and early board sidewalks.

Bottom Left: Morton McCarver came to Oregon in 1843 from Kentucky, founded the Linnton townsite to rival Portland.

Bottom Right: Peter Burnett, a Tennessee lawyer, came to Oregon in 1843, was McCarver's partner in founding Linnton.

Top: The *Columbia,* a steamship with auxiliary sails, began service to Portland and St. Helens in 1851.

Center: The *Goliah,* an early steamship on the Pacific Coast, visited Portland in 1851.

Bottom: The steamboat *Iris* ran on the Columbia River upstream from Portland in the 1860s. Henry Knighton was her captain.

The Portland proprietors announced that the *Gold Hunter* would henceforth run regularly, twice a month, between Portland and San Francisco. Two men who had bought small amounts of stock in the venture were put in charge aboard the vessel. One of these was T. A. Hall, who was made Captain. Prior to that, he had been captain of the sailing bark, *Ocean Bird,* one of the vessels in the service of Whitcomb's mills at Milwaukie. This was also the Captain Hall whom Editor Dryer had run afoul of, when he was impatiently awaiting the sailing vessel bringing his printing press. If Dryer discerned a sinister portent in the selection of this Captain, his forebodings were to be fully justified by later events. The other shareholder given office aboard the *Gold Hunter* was A. P. Dennison, who was made purser.

The *Gold Hunter* remained at Portland for about a week, then paddled down the river for San Francisco, with 20 passengers. She cleared out of the mouth of the Columbia on December 11th. She re-entered the Columbia on December 28th, bringing 56 passengers for Portland. On that trip, she arrived in the Columbia just 76 hours after leaving San Francisco, which in 1850 was considered a very fast voyage.

The passengers on that trip were so impressed with the *Gold Hunter* that several of them wrote a testimonial, which appeared in the *Spectator* over their names:

A Testimonial to Captain Hall, of the
Gold Hunter, on her First Trip under
His Command, from San Francisco to Portland

————————

The undersigned take pleasure in recommending her as a fast sailing and sea worthy steamer. They also tender their acknowledgements to Captain Hall

and the officers for their uniform kindness and courtesy. We also take pleasure in mentioning the Stew-
ard, for providing a table equal to that in a first
class hotel. We consider the introduction of the *Gold
Hunter*, as a regular trader between San Francisco
and Portland, as the dawn of a new era in the commercial prospects of Oregon.

The *Spectator* also, on its own behalf, printed a rather
quaint tribute to Captain Hall:

> ☞ Our thanks to Capt. T. A. Hall, of the steamer
> Gold Hunter, for late files of San Francisco papers.
> We shall endeavor to reciprocate such favors. We
> set Capt. Hall down as a clever fellow.

Just how clever he was, the Portland proprietors were
shortly to learn, to their cost.

The *Gold Hunter*, on that trip, reached Portland December 29th, remained till January 2nd, then left again
for San Francisco. However, she had to wait three days
at Astoria, for a storm to subside, before she could get
out over the bar. She was back again January 22nd, with
55 passengers for Portland. This time, the voyage up
took six days, because she "touched at Trinidad Bay"
[near present-day Eureka] to land passengers for the
new gold mines on the Klamath River.

Chapman, of the Portland Trio, was Agent for the
Gold Hunter. The advertisements he placed in the newspapers in early 1851 show the nature of the trade. For
example:

> W. W. Chapman, Agent for *Gold Hunter*, offers 200
> live fat pigs, suitable for roasts.

Some of the inconvenient details troubling a shipping
agent evidently annoyed lawyer Chapman, judging from
this peremptory warning in the *Spectator*:

> ### To W. H. WILDER
> SIR—Sundry boxes of yours, freighted per steamer *Gold Hunter,* are now in my charge at Portland. Unless the dues are paid forthwith, I will sell them to the highest bidder.
> W. W. Chapman
> Agent, Steamer Gold Hunter

Chapman the barrister could on occasion be a little irascible; he was once jailed for contempt of court because of the "unusually strong language" he used to express his opinion of a judge.

The *Gold Hunter* was back at Portland February 18th and again during the first week of March 1851. That, however, was her last trip. Then, the venture suddenly terminated in a costly debacle. The *Gold Hunter,* despite brave appearances, had been losing money. Also, she had some old debts against her which had not been fully revealed to the Portland proprietors. On her return to San Francisco in the second week of March, her ownership changed hands. Lownsdale-Coffin-Chapman had a very thin majority of the shares in the vessel, and that only when combined with the small interests of Captain Hall and Purser Dennison. The Portland Trio believed they had an understanding that, if any of the shares held by Oregonians were sold, they would only be sold to the other Oregon owners. However, in San Francisco, the minority stockholders there induced Hall and Dennison to sell out to them, thereby giving the San Franciscans just over 50 per cent of the ownership. The new owners, now having control, sold the *Gold Hunter* to cover part of her back debts. The Portlanders lost their entire investment in the venture. Coffin, especially, was hard hit; he was obliged to sell many lots in the

Portland townsite at bargain prices, in order to meet his losses.

Altogether, the *Gold Hunter* had made five trips to Portland. Though she had cost the Portland proprietors dearly, she had added to the evidence that steamers could reach Portland with ease and that Portland could provide adequate passenger traffic and cargoes for such vessels. However, even without the *Gold Hunter*, Portland did not entirely lack steamship service. The little *Sea Gull* was still steaming up and down the coast, and came to Portland a few times during 1851, although unpredictably. She carried both passengers and freight. In February 1852, however, the *Oregonian* printed an announcement of a sort which was sadly frequent in those days:

> The propellor *Sea Gull* cleared for Portland from San Francisco nearly a month ago, since which nothing has been heard of her. Fears are entertained for her safety.

Later, it was learned that the poor little *Sea Gull* had been "overcome by heavy seas, and beached at Humboldt, California." She was a total loss, but all hands were saved.

In March 1851, two Pacific Mail Steamship Company vessels, which were to be important in the navigation history of the Lower Willamette, arrived at Astoria. One was the steamship *Columbia*, the vessel in which Coffin had had an interest and which was built specially for the Oregon-San Francisco route. The other vessel was the steamboat *Willamette*, 390 tons, whose purpose would be to serve the towns on the Columbia and Willamette Rivers and to bring mail, passengers, and freight to Astoria to meet the *Columbia*. At this point in its plans, the P.M.S.Co. intended that its ocean vessels would come only to Astoria. There was some delay in making the *Willamette* ready for service on the river, however; she had come round the Horn under sail, and her side-paddles had to be installed.[5] During this period, the *Columbia* made a trip up the river to Portland, April 22, 1851.

Also, in the spring of 1851, one more steamship came up to Portland. She was the *Goliah*, a little vessel of 333 tons, which had just arrived on the Pacific Coast from New York. She entered the Columbia River April 9th, 3½ days from San Francisco, and reached Portland the next day. The *Oregonian* reported that "It is said the *Goliah* will continue as a regular packet between this place and San Francisco, making a trip every two weeks." The *Goliah* remained in the river four days and then, April 14th, cleared out of the Columbia for San Francisco. She did not return, despite the rumors the *Oregonian* had optimistically reported. Her owners were dissuaded from entering the Oregon trade by the P.M.S.Co's. larger and faster *Columbia*, now beginning regular service to Astoria, which would skim off the more profitable business.

None of the ocean steamers that entered the Willamette during 1850 and 1851 (the *Carolina, Massachusetts, Sea Gull, Gold Hunter, Columbia,* and *Goliah*) ever came above Portland, and there was little likelihood one ever would be seen at Milwaukie. However, Lot Whitcomb was not the sort of man to resign himself to defeat. Most, in fact nearly all, of the vessels coming into the Columbia and Willamette Rivers at this time were under sail, not steam. Of these sailing vessels, a number were coming to Milwaukie, though one had to admit that most of them stopped at Portland, or anchored at some other place farther down the river. But Whitcomb had been working on a plan which he hoped would change this, and enable Milwaukie to become a busier ocean port.

13. MILWAUKIE'S GLORY: THE STEAMBOAT "LOT WHITCOMB"

THE PROPRIETORS of Milwaukie and Portland all had reason to feel satisfied with the results of their missions to San Francisco in the spring and summer of 1850. Coffin and Chapman had done good work in promoting the future visits of steamships to Portland and had acquired editor T. J. Dryer and his press. Whitcomb had found the printers he needed. And he had opened an attack on a new front: he had purchased the machinery for a steamboat to run on the Willamette and Columbia Rivers. Further, he had found a trained engineer who agreed to come to Milwaukie to help build the steamboat and to be its Chief Engineer when it was put in service. The new recruit was Jacob Kamm, a valuable addition to the Milwaukie group and later a wealthy steamboat entrepreneur with the powerful Oregon Steam Navigation Co. Kamm was born in Switzerland, had received a diploma in engineering, and had been an engineer on Mississippi River steamboats. He crossed the plains to California in 1849 and was engineer on a steamboat running between San Francisco and the Sacramento River when Whitcomb offered him an even higher wage to come to Milwaukie. Kamm was then 27 years old.

Whitcomb also found in San Francisco a man to pilot his riverboat: Captain John C. Ainsworth. Ainsworth was born in Ohio and had become a pilot and captain on a Mississippi River steamboat before he responded to the call of gold in California. While on the Mississippi, he had worked with Mark Twain, who was then a riverboat pilot. Ainsworth was about to start as captain of a steamboat on the Sacramento River when Whitcomb offered him so much money ($300 a month) that he changed his plans. He was 28 years old. Like Kamm, he was an important reinforcement for Milwaukie. He later became a tycoon in river steamboating, railroading, and banking. It is an indication of Whitcomb's enthusiasm and persuasiveness that he could induce these able young men to leave the golden atmosphere of California to come to an unknown village in the forests of Oregon. But Whitcomb believed in Milwaukie, and, having already sold himself on its future, was able to transmit his confidence with convincing sincerity.

The machinery Whitcomb found for his steamboat had been brought to San Francisco to be installed in a boat on the Sacramento River. But Whitcomb saw that it was just what he wanted, and bought it before it had even been unloaded from the sailing ship in which it had just arrived. Once again, Whitcomb showed the prompt decisiveness, backed by a generous cash offer, which made him an effective proprietor. He had the ready money as a result of the profits he was making from his shipments of lumber and produce to California. Whitcomb paid $15,000 for the boat's machinery. Whitcomb, of course, was not working alone, but together with several associates, who also contributed capital and enterprise for Milwaukie's projects. One of these partners, Berryman Jennings, was with Whitcomb on this important trip to San Francisco.

The rival proprietors of Milwaukie and Portland arrived back in Oregon at about the same time, each well-satisfied in the happy thought that he had outdone the others. Chapman was one of 77 passengers who "came up" on the *Carolina*, which arrived at Portland July 15th, 1850. It must have been, for Chapman, a source of great satisfaction to have the steamer paddle right up to the dock at his own townsite. About two weeks later, Coffin, Whitcomb, and Jennings were fellow passengers on the *Carolina's* next trip. And there was another pertinent entry in the list of 37 passengers who "came up" on that trip: "Benjamin Stark and Servant." Stark was a young man who liked to live comfortably. And he had done so well, on the *Toulon*, in the gold fields, and with his speculation in the Portland townsite, that he could afford to do so.

That trip up from San Francisco took five days, and doubtless Coffin and Stark enjoyed many hours in conversation with their rivals, Whitcomb and Jennings, in the well-appointed lounge of the *Carolina*. Perhaps they kept demurely silent about their plans to begin publishing newspapers, which each hoped to issue before the other. But, as to Whitcomb's proposed river steamboat, he could not keep that a secret: its construction had already begun, in Kellogg's little shipyard at Milwaukie. Its keel had been laid in June, with confidence that Whitcomb's search at San Francisco for its machinery would be successful. And some of the specifications of the boat had been published in the *Spectator*.

As the rival townsite proprietors approached the Willamette, aboard the *Carolina*, they learned that the steamship would not be landing at Portland this time. This was the last trip of the *Carolina* to Oregon, the one on which the captain decided it would be safer to come only to Vancouver, because of low water in the Willamette. This must have disappointed and perhaps even embarrassed Coffin. From Vancouver, Coffin and the others had to proceed by small boat to Portland and Milwaukie. This, of course, was just what Whitcomb wanted. His own river steamboat would soon be able to connect with the mail steamers, wherever they might terminate, and if they chose not to come to Portland, Milwaukie would have the edge on its rival. Beyond that, Whitcomb had another plan for his steamboat: it would be able to tow sailing vessels.

A major difficulty for sailing vessels in a river was their lack of maneuverability. Helpless in the river current, unless there was enough wind to give them the momentum through the water that made them controllable, they often had to lie at anchor along the riverbank for days before they dared advance even a few miles. Furthermore, the narrowness of a river channel prevented their tacking into the wind, as they might do in open ocean, so that the wind had to be from the right direction. These difficulties made even more hazardous the numerous shallow bars in the Columbia and Willamette Rivers. Generally, there was enough water in the main channel for sailing vessels to get over most of these bars during all but the lowest stages of the river. The problem lay in keeping the vessel from drifting out of the channel. Whitcomb's steamboat would solve all these difficulties by carefully towing sailing vessels, wind or not, in the deepest channel.

The machinery for Whitcomb's new riverboat was brought up from San Francisco to Milwaukie on the bark *Louisiana* early in August. Kamm accompanied the machinery. Also on the same voyage were the two printers, Waterman and Carter. It was, indeed, a precious cargo for the Milwaukie proprietors. Evidently, Kamm, Waterman and Carter had an uncomfortable trip up the coast; they were among the signers of a joint letter of thanks to the *Louisiana's* captain, testifying to that "able and gentlemanly commander's untiring care for those of us who were sick." Until October 19th, when the *Desdemona* arrived with the printing equipment, Waterman and Carter joined the other Milwaukians working in Kellogg's shipyard on the new riverboat. Ainsworth came up on the P.M.S.Co's. steamship *California*, which brought 105 passengers to Astoria September 1st, after which he, too, joined the crew in the shipyard.

Milwaukie's steamboat was specially designed for convenience on the river. Powered by side paddle-wheels, rather than a propeller which would have required a deeper hull, she needed only about three feet of water. Yet she was 160 feet long. Her shallow draft was made possible by her width. She was broad in the beam—24 feet not counting the side wheels. The two paddle-wheels added nine feet more on each side, so that her over-all width was 42 feet. The huge paddle-wheels were 19 feet in diameter. At 300 tons, she was heavier than most of the ocean-going sailing vessels coming into the Willamette at the time and nearly as large as some of the steamships in the coastal trade in 1850 and 1851.[6]

Whitcomb's steamboat, taking shape on the riverbank at Milwaukie in the fall of 1850, was not the first river steamer to glide up and down the Willamette. That was the little riverboat which James Frost launched at Astoria in the spring of 1850. Her name was *Columbia*,[4] which led to some confusion since the P.M.S.Co. ocean steamship bore the same name. On her first voyage up the river, the little riverboat left Astoria at noon on July 3rd, reached Portland at 3 PM. July 4th, where she rested for two hours, and then went on to Oregon City, making those last 12 miles in three hours. She reached Oregon City at 8 P.M. on the Fourth of July, and a great celebration was held in her honor, adding a proud note to the day's patriotic festivities. On that trip, her passengers noticed, as the *Columbia* steamed past Kellogg's shipyard, the hull of Whitcomb's steamboat, already under construction even though Whitcomb himself was still in San Francisco looking for her machinery.

For six months, the *Columbia* had a monopoly, making trips between Oregon City and the various downstream townsites to Astoria, where she connected with the Mail Steamships. The riverboat's scheduled time between Portland and Astoria was 24 hours, and the fare was $25 per person or per ton of freight. Her regular schedule provided two trips each month between Oregon City and Astoria. At other times, she hauled freight and passengers on a non-scheduled basis, along the Willamette and up the Columbia to the Cascades.

The *Columbia* was hardly a match for Whitcomb's new boat, as the following figures show:

The *Columbia*		Whitcomb's Steamboat
90 feet	Length	160 feet
75 tons	Tonnage	300 tons
75 hp.	Horsepower	140 hp.
4 mph.	Speed (upstream)	14 mph.
$25,000	Cost	$80,000

Unlike the *Columbia*, Whitcomb's boat was fitted with berths and staterooms. Both were propelled by side paddle-wheels. But the *Columbia* lacked both the weight and power to be an effective towboat for sailing vessels.

Early in 1850, the *Spectator* was able to report that Whitcomb's steamboat was nearing completion:

> Milwaukie — A friend has informed us that the steamboat that is being built there has progressed rapidly; it is large and is a beautiful model. It will not only be a pride to its parent, but an ornament to the Territory.

The model for his steamboat, Whitcomb stated, was the design of "the first-class fast North River boats" on New York's Hudson River.

The momentous day of launching approached, but it brought with it a problem: the vessel had no name. Selecting a name turned out to be nearly as difficult as constructing the boat. The name "Milwaukie" they had already bestowed on the first small schooner they had built. Other suitable names, such as "Columbia," "Willamette," and "Oregon," had been preempted by others. Whitcomb decided to submit this baffling problem to the Legislative Assembly for decision. If Whitcomb had not had such a sincere and open personality, it might be suspected that he was plotting a townsite publicity stunt, but in his case that would seem to be an unfair presumption. The Legislative Assembly scheduled a public meeting, which was held at Oregon City. The *Western Star* reported the proceedings:

> At a meeting of the citizens of Oregon City, held by invitation, on the 6th [of December], for the purpose of naming the steamboat now being constructed at Milwaukie, Capt. William K. Kilborn was called to the chair, Asahel Bush appointed secretary, and A. L. Lovejoy, H. Campbell, W. W. Buck, Governor Gaines, and Captain Kilborn were appointed a committee to select a suitable name for the steamer. The committee retired and subsequently reported the name "Lot Whitcomb of Oregon."

Whitcomb wrote a letter, which he addressed to Governor John P. Gaines, acknowledging the selection of his name. It is written in the effusive, flamboyant style characteristic of the mid-Victorian era, and gives us another glimpse of Lot Whitcomb the man:

> "Your committee will first please accept my most unfeigned and sincere respects, and through you to the citizens and legislative assembly I beg leave to tender my hearty thanks for the honor they have done me. I can not but feel proud at this much of respect shown me. It always has been my earnest desire to keep pace with, and assist in forwarding any improvements proposed in this my adopted country, and rest assured the compliment you have paid me, in naming the Steamer 'Lot Whitcomb of Oregon,' will tend to add another impetus to my desires.
>
> Your ob't ser't.
LOT WHITCOMB"

With the ritual of selecting a name accomplished, the Milwaukie proprietors proceeded to organize a great celebration for launching day. The day itself was carefully chosen. If the little *Columbia* could have a gala reception at Oregon City on the Fourth of July, the *Lot*

Whitcomb should be christened on an even more impressive day: Christmas! Arrangements for the occasion included a banquet, a Ball, and a concert by the Vancouver Brass Band, comprised of musicians from the regiment of "Mounted Rifles" of the U.S. Army which had now supplanted Hudson's Bay Company at Fort Vancouver. The arrangements seem extravagant, but, on the frontier, few diversions were possible; public occasions were almost the only recreation.

The launching was described in the *Western Star* in its issue of the following day, December 26, 1850. Editor Waterman's picturesque account included these passages:

> The launching of the new and beautiful steamer, the product of the enterprise and energy of one of our most worthy citizens, naturally called together a large assemblage of people from the surrounding country. About 3 o'clock P.M., everything being in readiness, and a goodly number on board, she was cut loose from her fastenings, and slid down the stocks into the water like a meteor from the heavens. His excellency, Governor Gaines, christened her "LOT WHITCOMB of Oregon." Mayor Kilborn presented the beautiful set of colors, from the citizens of Oregon City to Captain Whitcomb, for the steamer. Captain Whitcomb responded in his usual easy and happy style.
>
> The splendid Vancouver Brass Band added much to the pleasantness of the occasion by playing, in most excellent taste, The Star-Spangled Banner, Hail Columbia, and Yankee Doodle.
>
> Evening: The Ball in honor of the launching came off in good order, and was numerously attended. The Vancouver Brass Band furnished excellent music, and supper was served in good style by Charles Sanborn of the Milwaukie Hotel.

The *Spectator*, reporting the launching, said "Christmas was truly a proud day for Milwaukie."

A ship launching is always a moment rich in portents, and this occasion was, unfortunately, marred by a tragic event that might well have been interpreted as an evil omen for Milwaukie. On the day of the launching there was a schooner, the *Merchantman*, lying at the sawmill at Milwaukie, loading lumber. The *Merchantman* had a cannon, which was loaned to the Committee on Arrangements, to be fired at the moment of launching, as a salute. When the time came, no one else was willing to fire the gun, so the captain of the *Merchantman*, Frederick Morse, took a heated rod of iron and touched off the powder. Evidently, in the enthusiastic desire to make a reverberating roar, they had over-charged the cannon, for it exploded and killed Captain Morse. The *Western Star* mourned the event, in an account which is interesting not only for its documentation but also as an example of nineteenth century journalism as composed by Waterman:

> Christmas Day: This morning commenced most beautifully—the atmosphere was pure and life-giving, and its temperature mild and lovely. The smiling sun of heaven shed its golden beams upon our beautiful valley. But one who commenced the day full of vigor and in manhood's prime, and who little suspected that danger lurked in his path, was destined to be snatched from among us in an instant. Capt. Frederick Morse, while in the act of touching fire to a cannon, was instantly killed by its bursting. Fragments were scattered about for some distance, injuring no one, however, but Capt. Morse. Thus it is ever with us mortals—truly "In the midst of life we are in death." But his tragic death was not able to stop the launching festivities.

However, though the day's subsequent events went off as planned, that sad incident hung like a cloud over the festivities for the rest of the day.

A few weeks after her launching, the new steamboat was ready for a trial run. Her performance was as spectacular as her careful construction and elaborate woodwork were impressive. Captain Whitcomb—and there was now another and more nautical reason to address him by a title which had initially come to him for having shepherded a fleet of prairie schooners across the plains— Captain Whitcomb was so pleased with the new boat that he gave a bonus of $1000 to the shipyard foreman who had been in charge of its construction. The *Western Star* rightfully called it "a handsome present."

Beginning in the first week of February 1851, the *Lot Whitcomb* was put on a regular run between Milwaukie and Astoria, touching at Portland,[7] St. Helens, Cowlitz (at the mouth of the Cowlitz River), and Cathlamet (also called "Burney's"). At Cowlitz, she connected with the COWLITZ RIVER CANOE LINE, then the only link, other than an ocean voyage, between the Willamette-Columbia River area and the settlements on Puget Sound. The *Lot Whitcomb's* schedule was designed to leave her substantial amounts of free time, during which she was available for towing sailing vessels. She also, occasionally, made a trip up the river towards Oregon City.

The usual fuel for the *Lot Whitcomb*, and other river steamboats, was wood, of which there was an abundance. However, Whitcomb showed his enterprise and imagination by experimenting with another fuel: coal. Coal had been found in Oregon Territory, in that portion of it now called Washington State, on the Cowlitz River. The *Oregonian*, in April 1851, reported:

> Oregon Coal—Captain Whitcomb informs us that he has thoroughly tested the Cowlitz coal, on a recent trip of the steamer *Lot Whitcomb,* and pronounces it A No. 1. A company is now making arrangements for a Coal depot at the mouth of the Cowlitz.

One of the reasons for Whitcomb's satisfaction with his steamboat was her speed. This was demonstrated on many occasions, one of the most dramatic being a race between the *Lot Whitcomb* and the steamship *Goliah*. The *Goliah* had entered the Columbia River, from San Francisco, April 9, 1851. The *Lot Whitcomb* happened to be at Astoria at the same time, and, since both vessels were coming up to Portland, it was inevitable that a "Steamboat Race" should suggest itself. The result of the race was reported in the *Oregonian*:

> Steamer Vs. Steamer: The steamer *Lot Whitcomb,* built in Oregon, and the steamer *Goliath,* from New York, had a trial of speed on Wednesday from Astoria to Portland. The *Goliath* has the strength of a noble steamer, and is considered a *fast boat,* yet the *Lot Whitcomb* exhibited the letters on her stern to the *Goliath*. Before they arrived at the mouth of the Willamette, passengers on the *Goliath* were trying out the boat's glasses, to see if they could read "Lot Whitcomb" at a distance of five miles ahead.

While the Lot Whitcomb was available to tow other sailing vessels, for a fee, Whitcomb was specially interested in having it ready to tow those coming to Milwaukie. He also arranged for a small boat to serve Oregon City from Milwaukie. Thus, he was able to provide passenger and freight service all along the river,

from Oregon City to Astoria, with a reliability thereto-
fore unknown. And his sailing vessels would be towed
whenever necessary. So enthusiastic was Whitcomb
about this arrangement that he announced it somewhat
prematurely. The following advertisement appeared in
the first issue of the *Western Star*, November 21, 1850:

NEW LINE
of
PACKET SHIPS
From Milwaukie to San Francisco

Bark OCEAN BIRD   T. A. Hall, Master
  " KEOKA   D. W. Hall, Master
  " LOUISIANA   G. W. Roberts, Master

No detention can happen in the river navigation,
on account of winds, to this line, as they will be
towed by a Steamer from and to the mouth of the
Columbia to Milwaukie.

                                    Lot Whitcomb.

The intimation, in this advertisement and in similar ones
placed at the same time in the San Francisco papers,
that the steamboat was already in service, caused some
misunderstandings. For example, when Dryer shipped
his printing equipment in the *Keoka*, it was long delayed
in coming up the river, as we have seen. In the alterca-
tion between the waiting editor and Captain Hall, Dryer
had remonstrated "to this lordly captain that it had been
represented to us that this vessel was to be towed up the
river by a steamer." Dryer pointed out to the captain
that, when he had arrived at Portland, "we learned to
our astonishment that the steamboat was *building* which
was to be employed, when completed, in towing vessels
up the river. The captain replied that the advertisement
did not say WHEN they were to use steam."

Despite his disgust at the misrepresentation and delay he had experienced at the hands of the "Milwaukie Line," with the consequence that the *Western Star* had come out ahead of his paper, Dryer was too honest a reporter to let it color his news accounts. In his first issue, December 4, 1850, he wrote this straightforward description of Milwaukie:

> Six miles above Portland is Milwaukie, which bids fair to compete with her sister town in enterprise and business. There is a good water power which is considerably improved already, and susceptible of still more improvement. A fine large steamer, designed for the navigation of the rivers, is being built at this place, and is now under a forward state of completion; we hope to see her in her native element.

Thus, the proprietors and promoters of Milwaukie had, at the beginning of 1851, several reasons for feeling optimistic. They had put a sawmill and flour mill in operation before Portland, though Portland had now equalized that advantage; they had got a newspaper started before Portland, though admittedly Editor Dryer was now very much in evidence; and they had parried the challenge of Portland's steamships with their own steamboat. Moreover, they had several other schemes afoot. The *Spectator*, in August 1850, had printed this note, "from a friend at Milwaukie":

> We have completed the following new roads: From this place to Oregon City, Molalla, Portland, and Tualatin Plains. As all these roads center at Milwaukie, the public are notified that they can cross the Willamette River at this place by a *free ferry*. There is now nearly framed a *warehouse*, four stories high, which will be ready to receive merchandise by the first of October.

Whitcomb clearly understood the importance of attracting the produce of the Tualatin Valley farmers. But the route was long and circuitous, and the ferry crossing inconvenient for horses and wagons.

In November 1850, the *Western Star* gave a brief summary of the accomplishments at Milwaukie: a good school, post office, tin shop, cabinet manufacturer, shoe shop, blacksmith, three stores, printing office, warehouse, three taverns, two sawmills, a flour mill, and a new sawmill and flour mill being built. In December 1850, the *Western Star* announced that twenty new residences had been commenced at Milwaukie within the preceding month.

Another account of the progress at Milwaukie, from a less biased source, appeared in the *Spectator* in March 1851. Editor Schnebly had taken a trip down the river to Astoria, and wrote:

> We came up broadside in front of Milwaukie. The captain gave us permission to go on shore for half an hour. We strolled out through brush and stumps, over hills and hollows, till we gained the office of the *Western Star*. Here we found Brother Waterman immersed in business, preparing his weekly treat for his subscribers. This was the first time we had been so low down on the Willamette River as Milwaukie, and truly were surprised to see so large a collection of houses—the growth of little more than a year.

With these impressive developments, it might have seemed that Milwaukie had good prospects in the battle for metropolitan supremacy. However, one fundamental issue had not yet been decided: Where was the Head of Navigation?

14. NAVIGATIONAL DIFFICULTIES

T HE "HEAD OF NAVIGATION" was a term the mere mention of which, along the Lower Willamette around 1850, caused tempers to flare. Arguments arose not only because personal interests were at stake, but also because the term was so imprecise. "Head of Navigation" only had meaning relative to the size of the vessel involved, and also the time of the year, for the depth of the Willamette varies greatly from season to season. Ocean-going vessels were certainly coming to Milwaukie. In 1850, there were as many as five of them in that port at one time. However, they were all small barks, or little schooners just adequate for the coastal lumber trade. Occasionally, one of these sailing vessels even went farther up the Willamette, to the Clackamas Rapids or right to Oregon City. Thus, proprietors with interests at Oregon City were allies with those at Milwaukie in arguing that the river was navigable above Portland for ocean vessels.

Numerous statements had been made, beginning at least as early as 1846, that Portland was the effective head of navigation on the Willamette. Captain Couch had, in the early 1840s, come to that conclusion. But there was a strong minority view. In December 1849, the *Spectator* had said, "Milwaukie may be said to be the head of ship navigation on the Willamette. We are assured that any vessel that can come into the river at all can come up to Milwaukie." Editor Schnebly had received those assurances from a man he identified as "our enterprising friend, Lot Whitcomb, Esq." Two issues later, in January 1850, Schnebly wrote:

> A few weeks since, we happened to make the re-mark that "We are assured that any vessel that can come into the Willamette at all can come up to Milwaukie." To this remark, exception has been taken, and from the bountiful shower of communi-cations that have fallen on us, we infer that there is some feeling abroad on the subject.

He then reproduced several of the letters he had re-ceived. They concerned primarily a sand and gravel bar at Ross Island. That bar, about three miles above the Portland townsite of 1850 and about three miles below Milwaukie, was the principal obstacle in navigating the river, above Portland, to Milwaukie.

The most important letter for the plaintiffs, attacking the statement the *Spectator* had made, was from Captain Couch himself, now residing at Portland, where he was a prosperous merchant and ship-owner. Couch wrote:

> Mr. Editor: I perceive that you have been led to believe that Milwaukie is at the head of ship naviga-tion; or rather that the Willamette is navigable for ships to that point. I think that with like pro-priety you may say that Oregon City is at the head of ship navigation, as ships have and may proceed thus far during the June rise of the Columbia, back water from that river making the Willamette navigable to Oregon City. But in ordinary low water, the bar [at Ross Island] has on it only about four feet of water. I have frequently observed Indians wading the river at that bar, and have crossed it on horseback myself at the same place.
>
> Jno. H. Couch

To Couch's letter was appended a testimonial:

> I reside opposite the bar mentioned, have followed boating over the same for several years, and I agree fully in the above statement of Captain Couch.
>
> Thomas Stephens

Editor Schnebly, when he received Couch's letter, knew that he had to print it; Couch was too prominent and influential a person to ignore, even if the editor had been tempted to put the letter aside. But he also knew that it might have a devastating effect on Milwaukie's prospects, since the *Spectator*, at that time Oregon's only newspaper, was a principal source of information about Oregon for shippers in California and "the States." Therefore, he generously got in touch with his "enterprising friend at Milwaukie," explained the contents of the letter he felt compelled to publish, and invited the Milwaukie proprietors to submit letters in rebuttal. When Couch's letter appeared in print, it was surrounded by several letters making a quite different case. One of them stated:

> The undersigned having, on the 5th of January 1850, made an examination of the Willamette River between Milwaukie and Portland, do hereby certify to all whom it may concern, that the *channel* is, in the shallowest places, never less than *fourteen feet deep*, at high tide, and that any vessel that can reach Portland may safely rely upon a sufficiency of water to float her to Milwaukie.
>
> > H. Luelling
> > Sam'l. Campbell
> > Jos. Kellogg

However, the three Milwaukians, in their enthusiasm, neglected to mention that, at the time they made their measurement, the Willamette was in flood. It was one of the highest floods the valley had ever experienced. That same issue of the *Spectator* stated, "Nearly all the mills in the Territory have been swept away or damaged." The previous issue of the *Spectator*, under the heading "Great Freshet," had reported that three of Oregon City's principal stores, as well as Moore's store at Linn City, had washed away. Though the flood crest had passed by January 5th, when the Milwaukians made their survey, the river was still abnormally high.

Another of the letters included some instructive details, in an account that, a century later, still rings convincingly with the writer's indignation:

> Mr. Editor: Understanding that someone has placed in your hands a communication which attempts, or pretends, to show that the Willamette is too shallow for navigation above Portland, I hereby present a brief statement of facts, to the end that the public mind may be set right in the matter. Sometime in the latter part of August 1849, the brig *Forrest* arrived at Portland from San Francisco, which vessel the proprietors of Milwaukie were concerned in—intending to load her with lumber. The said proprietors wishing, if possible, to load the vessel at their mill, two of them (Mssrs. Lot Whitcomb and Joseph Kellogg) together with myself, went down the river for the purpose of sounding the channel and piloting the vessel up.
>
> I cast the lead all the way down, and in the shallowest place, which is a short distance below the house of Mr. Stephens, I found 12 feet of water, the river at this time being very low.
>
> We then went on board the brig at Portland and represented the matter to Captain Williams. Captain Johnson, formerly Captain of the *Prince of Wales* in the employ of the Hudson's Bay Company, who was on board, having piloted the brig from the Columbia, stated he thought it would be impossible for the vessel to get up. He believed there was no more than seven feet at the place mentioned below Stephens'. The Captain was therefore unwilling to start up until he should sound the channel himself, which he accordingly did, and found

the depth of water the same as I reported, and expressed his willingness to take the vessel up, which he did without the least difficulty.

The vessel was loaded with lumber. In a few days she was ready to go out. Drawing something over ten feet water, she went down without the least difficulty. At Portland, we took on said Captain Johnson, to pilot the vessel to Baker's Bay. When opposite the head of Swan Island, we run aground, and, on sounding, found that we were very near the deepest water. After lying there near a day, we got off at high water. Within about a mile of the Columbia [Post Office Bar], we again run aground, Captain Johnson declaring that we were in the deepest water. Both he and Captain Williams admitted, what, of course, was evident to anyone, from these facts, that any vessel that could get to Portland could get to Milwaukie.

Now, sir, I have given a plain unvarnished statement of facts, not with a view to self interest, for I have no interest in the proprietorship of Milwaukie or of any other town in Oregon. And before winter ends, I will be far up the valley in the peaceful occupation of tilling the soil, uncontaminated by the spirit of rivalry which is forever at work distracting the quiet of the inhabitants of these embryo cities. I repeat, that a sense of *truth and justice* alone has impelled me to make the foregoing statement.

Wm. J. Berry

The argument continued throughout 1850. But the idea that Portland was as far up the river as a prudent captain should come, unless his vessel was quite small, had been firmly planted by Couch, not only in his letter of January 1850 but earlier. And his view was seconded by Captain Nathaniel Crosby, Jr., another well-known New Englander. Crosby, in a letter to the Oregon Territory's delegate to Congress, Samuel Thurston, written in August 1849, had called Portland "the head of navigation for shipping." In December 1850, even Governor

Gaines, in a prepared message, intimated that Portland was the head of navigation. He said:

"It will be greatly to the advantage of the people of Oregon that certain towns should be designated as ports of entry, the most prominent of which would seem to be Portland, it being the nearest point to Oregon City accessible to large ships."

Events, as well as public statements, gradually began to tip the scales against Milwaukie. In December 1850, Editor Dryer, probably with a wry smile, was able to print this item:

> ☞ We learn that the bark SUCCESS is hard upon a rock in the river, between here and Milwaukie.

In fact, Editor Dryer had a double reason to chortel: the *Success* had aboard, among other cargo, supplies of paper and ink for the *Spectator*.

In 1851, after more river steamboats began to appear on the Willamette, there were further difficulties with the bar between Portland and Milwaukie. In December, for instance, the *Spectator* reported:

> We regret to learn that the steamboat *Washington*, when opposite Stephens' Point, broke a propellor by its striking upon the bottom of the river, while over the bar that is in the stream at that place.

In January 1852, this item appeared:

> Aground: The steamboat *Willamette* got hard aground a few days since, while attempting to get the bark *Mary Melville* off from a bar in the river about three miles above Portland.

Whitcomb and his colleagues had made a valiant effort to bring more ocean vessels to Milwaukie, or at least to keep their own sailing fleet in service. And small sailing vessels did continue to find their way, carefully and slowly, up to Milwaukie throughout the 1850s, though their visits were less and less frequent. The ships coming into the river were larger, now. Steamships were beginning to take all of the passenger traffic and an increasing share of the freight, and none of them ventured above Portland. In fact, there was some doubt whether even Portland would be served by them, a question which was to give the Portland Trio some anxious days. So, during the 1850s, though Milwaukie remained a stop for riverboats, it was gradually abandoned as an ocean port.

15. MILWAUKIE: DECLINE AND FALL

TODAY, WHEN WE SEE dredging machinery maintaining a 40-foot channel from Portland to the sea, and an 8-foot channel from Portland to Oregon City, we might suppose that Whitcomb could have tried to dig out the Ross Island bar. But, at that time, there was no equipment that could do such a job. Even a much smaller problem, excavating the Clackamas Rapids to a depth of only 2½ feet, to accommodate light riverboats appearing on the Willamette in the 1850s, plagued Oregon City for a decade. To dredge and maintain a channel adequate for steamships or large sailing vessels to come to Milwaukie in safety at all seasons was beyond the capabilities of any machinery, or any capitalist, on the Pacific Coast in 1851. Certainly, no capitalist would have invested in such a project, since directly below Ross

Island was Portland, which could offer more inducements to shipping—wharves, warehouses, markets, and
freight—than Milwaukie and which steamships could
reach by a natural channel.

Even if Whitcomb had been quixotic enough to dream
of dredging, it was out of the question for another reason: by early 1851, our enterprising friend was virtually
bankrupt. Whitcomb, like any speculator convinced that
he has a good thing, had stretched his resources to the
breaking point. But Fate had not smiled. Beginning in
the spring of 1851, Milwaukie's fortunes began to decline
with a rapidity almost as surprising as that with which
they had risen during the preceding two years.

The first blow, which came two weeks before the omi-
nous explosion of the cannon at the Christmas Day
launching, was reported by this newspaper item:

> We have learned with regret that the sawmill of
> Mr. Lot Whitcomb at Milwaukie has burned down.
> The fire was discovered at too late an hour to arrest
> its progress.

There was still another sawmill at Milwaukie, and Whitcomb's was eventually rebuilt, but the lost income was
sorely missed. The income Whitcomb needed was further reduced by a decline in lumber prices in California.
Many mills had started up, to take advantage of the
almost piratical profits, and at the same time this competitive supply was increasing, the period of most desperate demand had passed. It was no longer possible to
dump a pile of rough boards on the beach at San Francisco and find frantic buyers pressing forward with
handfuls of gold, outbidding one another.

Another blow to Whitcomb and his associates was the
discovery that the *Lot Whitcomb* was a very expensive

boat to operate. Certainly, she was big, beautiful, and powerful; but her operating expenses were on an equally grand scale. She did not make the profits her proprietors expected and needed. In 1851, Capt. Ainsworth, whom Whitcomb had promised a salary of $300 a month, had not yet been paid; he was persuaded to accept $2000 worth of stock in the steamboat venture in lieu of wages.

Furthermore, steamboat competition on the river was increasing. Early in May 1851, a little makeshift steamboat called *Hoosier No. 1* began running between Portland and Oregon City. Later that month, another and better equipped steamboat arrived, the *Black Hawk*. She was imported by Abernethy & Co., of Oregon City, and put in regular service between that town and Portland, as described in this newspaper advertisement:

> REGULAR TRIPS
>
> THE BLACK HAWK, Charles Clark, Commander, will run regularly between Oregon City and Portland—leaving the first named place in the morning and returning the same day. The travelling public are assured that strict punctuality, as to the time of starting, will be observed.
>
> Oregon City, May 29, 1851

Another competitor on the Portland-Oregon City run was the *Eagle*, a small steamboat of which Richard Williams was captain. Since Williams was also the entire crew—fireman, engineer, and deckhand—this was an efficient operation. At a passenger fare of $5 one way, Williams made a substantial amount of money. The *Eagle's* cost and income were in a much happier balance than those of the *Lot Whitcomb*. Williams later became president of Portland's First National Bank.

These little steamboats were skimming off the profits from the *Lot Whitcomb's* operations between Portland

and Milwaukie. On the longer run downstream to Astoria, formidable competition appeared when the *Willamette* began running. This was the large steamboat, about the size of the *Lot Whitcomb* and even more luxurious, which the Pacific Mail Steamship Company had brought from the East Coast to carry passengers and freight on the river, connecting with the company's ocean-going steamships at Astoria. In April 1851, the *Oregonian* announced that "The steamboat *Willamette* will soon take her place in the 'line,' and thereby form a continuous line of direct steam navigation from this city to New York, via Panama."

Whitcomb and company, with faltering income and short of capital, were forced to make a painful sacrifice. It was announced in the *Spectator* in June 1851:

> A controlling interest in the elegant Steamer *Lot Whitcomb* has been purchased by the people of this City [Oregon City]. She is now lying at our wharf, for the purpose of undergoing a thorough repairing for the better accommodation of the traveling public.

The principal stockholder in the *Lot Whitcomb* was now Abernethy & Company. Editor Waterman reported the sale of Milwaukie's greatest glory in these words:

> The fast sailing Steamer *Lot Whitcomb* we understand has been purchased by a company of capitalists at Oregon City. She is now undergoing repairs, and will be finished up in style. We are glad to learn that Captain Ainsworth is to be retained as Commander.

The *Lot Whitcomb* continued to run on the river until 1854. She was still an expensive boat to operate, however, and when the increasing number of steamships made her less in demand as a tugboat for sailing vessels, her Oregon City owners sold her to a California enterprise. The *Oregonian* in August 1854 reported:

> ☞ The steamer *Lot Whitcomb* left on Saturday last [August 12] for San Francisco. She has been purchased for an opposition boat against the organized steamboat monopoly of California [the California Steam Navigation Company]. Captain Flavel took her safely over the bar to sea . . . when she was taken in tow by the steamship *Peytona* . . . Captain Ainsworth accompanied her down. We shall look with anxiety for the news of her safe arrival at San Francisco.

The departure of the *Lot Whitcomb* evoked a sentimental reverie in Editor Waterman, who wrote:

> We are informed that the Steamer *Lot Whitcomb* has been sold to a California company and will shortly leave the Columbia to ply on the Sacramento River. We well recollect the first stroke of work we did in Oregon was on this boat, when, near four years ago, we arrived and were impatiently waiting for the arrival of our printing materials. It was a noble enterprise and she has done the country a good service.

In California, the *Lot Whitcomb* was re-named *Annie Abernethy* and put on the Sacramento-San Francisco run, where she served for many years.

Even the sale of the *Lot Whitcomb* was not Milwaukie's worst humiliation, however. That was the loss of her newspaper. The loss, calamity enough, was exacerbated by the newspaper's actual defection to Milwaukie's mortal enemy, Portland. This embarrassing move, regarded by Whitcomb and his loyal colleagues as little less than apostasy, came about in this way. Early in 1851, when Whitcomb had found it inconvenient to pay Captain Ainsworth his accumulated back wages and instead gave him a share in the steamboat, he also could not pay the wages of his editor and printer. So Whitcomb handed over to them, in lieu of wages, the ownership of the *Western Star* and its plant. The issue of February 27, 1851 removed Whitcomb's name from the masthead, and contained this letter from the ex-publisher:

> Having entered into arrangements by which the *Western Star* establishment, with the dues of the same, have passed into the hands of Messrs. Waterman and Carter, who have been engaged in the office since its commencement, I take this opportunity to recommend them and the paper to my friends and the public generally.
>
> Lot Whitcomb

During that spring, when the decline in the affairs of Milwaukie became pronounced, Waterman and Carter began to fear that their paper, even with its commercial printing business, might not be able to survive at that location. It is perhaps the most eloquent testimonial that could be given to the triumph of Portland over Milwaukie at this time that Waterman and Carter decided to move their plant to Portland, even though there was already a vigorous rival entrenched there. One dark night, at the end of May, they loaded their press and equipment on a flatboat and were paddled down to Portland. They chose to make their exit as inconspicuous as possible. Though they owned the equipment and had a legal right to do with it as they pleased, they wanted to avoid an open collision with the citizens of Milwaukie, who, indeed, were aghast and indignant when they found what had happened.

At Portland, Waterman and Carter changed the name of their publication to the Oregon Weekly *Times*, though they continued the numbering of the issues from the first one they had put out at Milwaukie. The first issue of the *Times* appeared June 5, 1851. Their explanation for the move was given in a simple, one-sentence statement:

OUR REMOVAL TO PORTLAND

In removing from Milwaukie to Portland, we have been guided by those considerations which govern all business men.

They had concluded that the commercial future lay not with Milwaukie but with Portland. Editor Dryer welcomed them in one of his more genial passages:

The organ of the Democratic Party has moved to Portland, and has appeared under a new name, Oregon Weekly *Times*. There is a moderation and manliness about the *Times* that we admire. . . . Success to the *Times* in everything save politics.

Lot Whitcomb, remaining at Milwaukie, now had to get his news through papers published at Oregon City or Portland. And, from the waterfront of his languishing townsite, he could watch his namesake—the "capitalists of Oregon City" had retained her name—paddling sedately up and down the river. However, he continued to engage in numerous public-spirited activities. He entered politics—he had earlier been a legislator in Illinois—and, in 1852, was elected to the House of Representatives. In that election, he was one of three representatives chosen from Clackamas County; all were Whigs. In the next Territorial election, in June 1854, Whitcomb did not seek re-election—wisely, since the Democrats swept the field. However, in November of that year, one of the Democrats, who had just been elected representative from Clackamas County, resigned, and a special election was scheduled to replace him.

Whitcomb announced himself a candidate, not as a Whig or Democrat but as an "Independent," a role congenial to a man of his stalwart individualism. In the newspapers, he placed an advertisement which reveals his political style and his view of the issues:

> To the People of Clackamas County: I offer myself as an independent candidate for the office of Representative, believing justice has not been done to our county. I will, if elected, try to make the Legislature remember that there IS such a county, which is entitled to consideration. Its rights and just claims never have been and I trust never will be bartered away by *me*, however slightly they may be regarded by my opponents. I am heartily opposed to any division of the county. My past services in your behalf are a guarantee of my future efforts, and I hope, if I am elected, you will never be ashamed of or regret your choice.
>
> Lot Whitcomb,
> Milwaukie

The Democrat organization put up A. L. Lovejoy. A second Democrat, James Loomis, representing another faction of the party, also entered the contest. The Whigs nominated Samuel Barlow, but Barlow withdrew, so that Whitcomb received most of the Whig vote. The election results were announced in the Democrat[8] Party organ, the *Statesman*, which added these labels after the names:

Lovejoy, Democrat and Anti-"Know-Nothing" 264
Whitcomb, "Know-Nothing," and receiving
   the Whig vote 206
Loomis, independent Democrat........................... 33

The Democrat majority in that election in November 1854 in Clackamas County reflected the origins of a majority of Oregonians at that time: the midwest, border

States, and the South. The "Know-Nothing" Party was a national political group of the 1840s and 1850s that emphasized "native Americanism." Its inner councils had some resemblance to a secret organization, and the party derived its name from the fact that its leaders, when asked questions, would often dodge the issues by simply replying "I don't know." Out in the Oregon Territory, the national policies of the "Know-Nothing" Party were less important. When the term was used, it was more as a temporary label around which could rally all those who opposed the Democrats. Many who voted "Know-Nothing" had been Whigs, who were politically homeless now that their own party, nationally, had been torn to pieces by dissension over the slavery issue. Though the *Statesman* labeled Whitcomb a "Know-Nothing," newspaper records do not show that he endorsed the rather narrow and intolerant views of some of the members of the party in the East.

After his defeat in 1854, and amidst the political party chaos as the Whigs and "Know-Nothings" disintegrated and the Republican Party had not yet formed, Whitcomb made a further shift in affiliation. In 1856, we find him listed as one of the delegates from Milwaukie to the Clackamas County Democrat Convention.

Whitcomb, despite his financial reverses, remained the generous man he was. In December 1851, he presented to the newly-organized Episcopal Church at Milwaukie two lots and a partially-finished building in which he had invested $1000 and which had been intended for a duplex. The Episcopalians engaged a carpenter to complete the building as a church. This church is today the oldest church building still in use in Oregon. However—symbolic of Milwaukie's defeat a century previously—it was moved down to Portland on a barge in 1961, where is rests in a riverside park, still in use for public services.

In 1852, Whitcomb undertook a humanitarian project: the relief of immigrants who had become stranded that fall between northeastern Oregon and The Dalles. He contributed money, and solicited money from others, to buy flour and other supplies, which he then personally took out to the suffering immigrants. Many diaries written by the pioneers of 1852 tell of meeting Whitcomb, in entries such as this: "Lot Whitcomb has provisions, but none to sell, but gives to all he finds in want and who are unable to buy." One of the immigrants Whitcomb helped at this time was Charles Stevens, to whom Whitcomb gave ten pounds of flour. Perhaps because of Whitcomb's assistance to him, Stevens chose to settle at Milwaukie. However, he only remained there about a year, and his principal reason for moving points up another handicap Milwaukie had: malaria. Sometimes called ague or intermittent fever in the mid-nineteenth century, when its nature and transmission were not yet understood, malaria had been a serious disease in the Willamette Valley since about 1829. It was endemic here as recently as the 1920s, and the anopheles mosquitoes capable of transmitting the disease are still numerous in the Willamette Valley. In the 1850s, the Oregon newspapers contained many advertisements for medicines to cure malaria. Among them was "Dr. Broy's Great Tonic Elixir, The Safest and Most Certain Cure for Ague and Fever, and the Bilious Fevers of Oregon." Malaria, or ague as it was called, was particularly prevalent at Milwaukie. Charles Stevens, whom Whitcomb had assisted along the immigration route, wrote in 1853 in a letter from his home at Milwaukie:[9]

"This place is one of the greatest ague holes in the Territory. There is the river on the west and two mill ponds on the south side and two on the north side of it, beside a small stream, large enough for a tannery, that comes in from the east into the town. This stream comes from a spring that is only a few steps from Mr. Whitcomb's door."

In December 1853, Stevens complained in another letter about Milwaukie's unhealthy location:

"We think of moving to Portland in a short time; we think we can get more work there than we can here. I can get nothing to do here, only when vessels are loading here, and this place is the most unhealthy of any place I know of on the river, or in the country."

Two months later, Stevens did in fact move to Portland.

Whitcomb, however, continued loyally to live at Milwaukie. In 1853, he began thinking about launching a new townsite, in southwestern Washington on Willapa Bay, and let his imagination contemplate the possibility of a railroad from there to Puget Sound. But that venture remained a vision. Among other activities, he was interested in a project to construct a railroad from Portland to Eugene, via Milwaukie, but no railroad was built during his lifetime. He was an insurance agent for the "North American Mutual Insurance Company" and he was also named "Special Indian Agent."

In March 1857, Lot Whitcomb died suddenly of an acute illness which was variously reported as "bilious cholic" or "inflammation of the bowels." The true nature of Whitcomb's illness is now only conjecture. However, the same issue of the newspaper that told of his death also reported several deaths from typhoid fever in the Willamette Valley upstream from Milwaukie. It seems probable, from the circumstances and symptoms, that Whitcomb was a victim of typhoid. Accurate diagnosis of typhoid fever, like malaria, was not always possible in the 1850s. Whitcomb was 50 years old at the time of his death.

The Oregon Weekly *Times* reported Whitcomb's death "at his residence, Milwaukie, very suddenly of bilious colic. Capt. Whitcomb leaves a widow and four daughters." Editor Waterman at the conclusion of the obituary added a personal note:

> Captain Whitcomb was our early friend and a man we know to have possessed a most generous nature. We may no more look upon his noble brow, nor listen to his agreeable conversation.

The *Oregonian* carried a two-line death notice, but nothing more. However, Editor Dryer did use the occasion to get in a dig at Waterman and the *Times*. Waterman had been flying the flag on his office at half-mast, out of respect for Whitcomb, and Dryer wrote this note:

> HALF-MAST—Some extraordinary "occasion" must have occurred at the *Times* office, as they have floated the "stars and stripes" at half-mast for several days. Perhaps the editor is mourning over some misfortune, the result of misplaced affection, or plighted faith on the part of his political admirers. . .

Since it can hardly be supposed that Dryer was unaware of Whitcomb's death, his own paper having printed the annnouncement and Portland being such a small village at the time, this must be another illustration of the fact that no holds were barred in the vendettas which Oregon editors carried on so gleefully in the 1850s.

By the summer of 1851, it had become clear that Milwaukie had lost out to Portland in the battle to become the Metropolis. The reasons for Milwaukie's defeat were also the issues that would be contested in the next round of battle, between Portland and new rivals downstream.

The most important reason for Milwaukie's defeat was her lack of an adequate river channel. Secondly, Milwaukie was not readily accessible to the farmers of the Tualatin Valley. Not only was the trail to Milwaukie long and arduous, but, having finally reached the riverbank opposite Milwaukie, the farmers faced a ferry crossing which was inconvenient for horses and wagons. The importance of access to the Tualatin Valley lay in the fact that it was the most densely-settled agricultural area near the Lower Willamette. Early settlers had been attracted there by its rich valley soil and by the fact that much of it was grassy prairie, without forests and easy to plow. On the east side of the river, the land was heavily forested and less inviting. Above Oregon City, the main Willamette Valley had the attractive features of the Tualatin Valley, but settlers there did not influence the location of the ocean port, since their produce had to be sent down by bateau in any case, as they were not within wagon distance of ocean shipping.

A third handicap confronting Whitcomb's townsite was that the terrain at Milwaukie was constricted. Building was only possible on the east bank, and there, no broad plain invited expansion. Across the river, the hills came down precipitously to the river, allowing few sites for buildings. Portland, by contrast, was at the point where the valley first widened out to provide a broad, flat area on both sides of the river suitable for easy building. Fourthly, while Whitcomb was well endowed with energy, imagination, and enterprise, he did not have the large supply of financial capital which the Portland Trio had pooled together. Finally, there was the problem of the unhealthiness of Milwaukie's damp site.

As a result of these difficulties, Milwaukie's day of ascendancy was brief. At the beginning of 1850, she had momentarily surged ahead of Portland in population, with about 500 inhabitants to Portland's 300. A year later, Milwaukie's population was still about 500, but Portland's had reached about 900, of whom half were immigrants of 1850 who had decided to settle at Portland. By 1860, Portland's population was 2900 and Milwaukie's 180.

With the aptly symbolic move of Milwaukie's newspaper to Portland, in June 1851, the battle was over. But there was no exultant shouting at Portland, because, though Whitcomb and Milwaukie had been relegated to a subsidiary role, another and more serious rival had appeared downstream.

16. RIVAL PROPRIETORS DOWNSTREAM

COMPETITION from downstream did not become acute for Portland until just about the time that her upstream rival, Milwaukie, had been decisively vanquished. Therefore, the Portland Trio did not have to divide their attention and resources by a war on two fronts simultaneously. Though no action, of a nature to alarm the Portlanders, occurred at the downstream townsites prior to 1850, the claims had been established several years earlier. These downstream claims, and their proprietors, were:

Location: *Proprietors:*

Linnton   Peter H. Burnett and Morton M. Mc-
               Carver

St. Helens   Capt. Henry M. Knighton and William H.
               Tappan

Milton   Capt. Nathaniel Crosby, Jr., and Thomas
               H. Smith

St. Johns   James Johns

Linnton. Peter H. Burnett came to Oregon from Tennessee, in 1843, aged 36. He was a lawyer, and he set up his office at Oregon City. He was prominent in the Provisional Government from 1844 to 1848, and served as a legislator and judge. As a Southerner, he helped add the Democrat tone to Oregon politics of that time. Morton M. McCarver, another Southern Democrat, from Kentucky, also came to Oregon in 1843. He, too, was 36 years old. Like Burnett, he was active in the Provisional Government, as a legislator and as "Commissary General" in the Rogue River Indian war. Before coming to Oregon, he had founded a townsite in Iowa.

The year after their arrival in Oregon, Burnett and McCarver took out their claim at Linnton. They named it in honor of Senator Linn, of Missouri, in recognition of his efforts to provide free land for settlers in Oregon. The location they chose was a proof of their astute discernment: it was at the Willamette River end of an old Hudson's Bay Company cattle trail across the hills to the Tualatin Valley. In 1845, they built a small warehouse at Linnton and induced the Provisional Government, in which they were both active, to improve the cattle trail. That year, the Provisional Government appointed three commissioners to survey and mark out a roadway 30 feet

wide, along the route of the trail, from Tualatin Plains
to Linnton. Burnett and McCarver, appreciating what
was a key issue in the battle among the Willamette townsites, wanted to attract the wheat from the Tualatin
farmers to a point where it could be put aboard ocean
vessels. Burnett said, "I have no doubt that this place
will be the great commercial town of the Territory."
However, both Burnett and McCarver continued to live
at Oregon City; they were absentee promoters of Linnton. It is a further indication of their political connections
that, by 1846, they had persuaded "Twality" County to
acquire their warehouse.

Unfortunately for Linnton's proprietors, the route to
it from the Tualatin Plains was long, steep, tortuous, and
almost impassable for loaded wagons. They tried to improve it, but it would have taken more capital than they
had to make a good road at that location. Even today,
the paved road that follows that route is slow and difficult for automobiles. Some wheat was shipped from
Linnton, but it was never a serious threat to the other
townsites. Lt. Howison, of the U.S. Navy Schooner
Shark, who visited Oregon in 1846, wrote of Linnton:

"This site was selected by a copartnership of gentlemen as the most natural depot for the produce of the
well-settled Twality Plains, and a road was opened over
the ridge of hills intervening between the plains and the
river. Linnton contains only a few log houses. Its few
inhabitants are very poor, and severely persecuted by
musquitos day and night. Not one of its proprietors re-
sides on the spot, and its future increase is, to say the
least, doubtful."

Two years later, a minister visiting Oregon summa-
rized Linnton in one crisp sentence in his diary: "Linn-

ton is small and will not be large." A year later, in July 1849, a soldier travelling by boat from Fort Vancouver to Oregon City wrote in his journal this epitaph: "Linnton is deserted." Its few residents had sought to improve their lot in the California gold mines. Burnett himself, indeed, was one of the first Oregonians to respond to the call of the gold. In September 1848, he left Oregon City, as "Captain" of the first party ever to drive wagons between Oregon and California. Previous travellers had moved on foot or horse. Burnett remained in California, and it is a spectacular tribute to his abilities that, in a short time, he became the first American governor of California. McCarver, too, left Oregon at the time of the "gold rush," later participating in the founding of Sacramento and Tacoma. Evidently townsite promotion was an interesting experience which, once tasted, could become a habit. But Linnton was not a success. Its road over the hills was too difficult. Its proprietors lacked capital. Not even deigning to live at their townsite, they seemed, besides, to lack enterprise and determination, certainly when compared to Whitcomb or Coffin. In addition, the topography at Linnton was adverse; at that point, the hills come down precipitously to the river, leaving only a narrow shelf for building. Portland, by contrast, was on a wide, gentle slope, where the hills curved away from the river, leaving a large area for expansion. The only asset Linnton had was accessibility for ocean vessels, in which respect it was somewhat superior to Portland, being below the Swan Island bar.

St. Johns. Before moving downstream to the more serious rivals, we can briefly note St. Johns, located just across the river from Linnton. Its parent was a man named James Johns, described variously as "a hermit and

recluse," "old Jimmy Johns," and "Saint Johns." Johns
left Missouri in the spring of 1841 for California. He
spent two years in the Sacramento Valley, unaware of
the gold lying at his feet which would convulse the nation six years later, and then, in May 1843, came north
with a party of Hudson's Bay Company employees to
Fort Vancouver. In 1844, under the spell of Burnett's
optimism, he settled at Linnton, where he bought a town
lot and helped build the warehouse being erected there.
In 1847, he filed a claim on the square mile just across
the river from Linnton. There, by 1850, Johns had laid
out some lots and was operating, in a quiet way, a country store. By 1851, there were about a dozen families
living in the vicinity. In 1852, he established a ferry—a
rowboat—across the Willamette between his claim and
Linnton. This was the old Hudson's Bay Company route
from Fort Vancouver to the Tualatin Valley, which, after
crossing the river, followed the cattle trail at the foot of
which Linnton had been located. Johns' name is, in some
later accounts, spelled without the "s"; however, in the
advertisement which he himself placed in the *Oregonian*
concerning his ferry, his name is plainly spelled "James
Johns." The *Oregonian*, in May 1886, reported that
"James Johns, the founder of St. Johns," had been found
dead in his bed by some neighbors. He was 77 years old
and "left considerable property." St. Johns was even less
a competitive threat to Portland than Linnton. Its proprietor lacked both capital and enterprise, it was located
on the wrong side of the river for the farmers of the
Tualatin Valley, and the terrain at the site was steep and
difficult for building.

St. Helens. The principal proprietor of St. Helens was
Captain Henry M. Knighton. Knighton came to Oregon

in a wagon train that left Missouri in April 1845. There were 293 persons in the wagon train. Though Knighton was not the leader, he had enough responsibilities on the trip to acquire the sobriquet "Captain," by which title he was being addressed when they arrived at Oregon City. Among his other duties on the trip was that of driving 30 loose cattle. "Captain" Knighton, as he continued to be called, was 25 years old when he reached Oregon. Within a few years, he was a Captain in a fuller sense of the word, as master of a vessel sailing between the Columbia River and California.

Knighton had ambition, energy, and enterprise. He quickly made friends and achieved position and status in the frontier town. It is an indication of his bearing and ability that Governor Abernethy appointed him "Marshal" of the Provisional Government within four months after his arrival at Oregon City. By that time, he also had married (his wife was Elizabeth Martin, of Yamhill County), and had opened a hotel, and had begun operating a ferry capable of transporting horses. He placed an advertisement for his hotel in the first issue of the *Spectator*, February 5, 1846:

CITY HOTEL
By H. M. Knighton
Oregon City
The City Hotel is undergoing repairs and the proprietor feels safe in saying that when completed, his customers will feel more comfortable. His table shall not be surpassed in this Territory. Those who favor him with a call from the west side of the river will receive horse ferriage free.

Later that month, Captain Knighton gave a "Ball" at his City Hotel. The occasion was to celebrate Washington's Birthday. Knighton, in a chivalrous gesture, made it an international event by inviting the officers of the British Sloop-of-War *Modeste*, then stationed at Fort Vancouver. This was several months before the signing of the treaty which determined the Canadian boundary, and Oregon was still under joint jurisdiction of Britain and the U.S. The "Ball" could not be held exactly on Washington's Birthday, however, for a reason quite sufficient in that pious age. As the *Spectator* explained, the 22nd fell upon the Sabbath; hence, the gala event would take place the following Tuesday. The *Spectator* later reported that the "Ball" had been a great success. An excerpt from that "news item" reveals something not only about the era but about nineteenth-century journalism:

WASHINGTON BALL

I was apprehensive there would be a failure of attendance, from a report being circulated there was to be ardent spirits served out. No one showed any signs of intoxication, and though the room was filled, all went on smoothly and agreeably, much to the credit of Mr. K. and lady, who left nothing undone that would contribute to the happiness of their guests. There were three officers of H.B.M.S. *Modeste* present.

The British officers reciprocated the hospitality of Captain Knighton, who was listed among those attending "A Theatre" aboard the *Modeste* three months later.

Knighton again showed his pleasure in playing the generous host on the occasion of Oregon City's Fourth of July celebration in 1846. The celebration included a public procession which, the *Spectator* reported, "terminated at the City Hotel, where a public dinner was prepared by Capt. H. M. Knighton, proprietor, by order of the committee on arrangments, which was free for all."

Knighton was Sergeant-at-Arms of the House of Representatives of the Provisional Government, meeting at Oregon City in 1846. In December 1846, he was elected "Marshal" under the Provisional Government, his previous appointment to that Territorial office having been made to fill a vacancy. He also, it appears, added to an already busy schedule by doing construction work: the appropriations voted by the Legislature in December 1846 included "$32.12 for pay to H. M. Knighton, for repairs done upon the Jail." The pay for such Territorial jobs as "Marshal" was nominal, just enough to cover out-of-pocket expenses. The financial statement of the Provisional Government for 1847 showed that Knighton's pay that year as "Marshal" was $32. In June 1848, Knighton was re-elected "Marshal." However, by that time he was no longer living at Oregon City, but was coming up for Legislative sessions from his new townsite down the river.

During 1846, Knighton had visited an undeveloped claim which later became St. Helens. He was impressed by its potentialities—townsites and their promotion had become a major topic of conversation along the Lower Willamette—and he acquired it from the original claimant, Bartholomew White. At the end of 1846, he sold his ferry and hotel businesses at Oregon City. In December 1846, he placed this advertisement in the *Spectator*:

All those who have accounts with H. M. Knighton for ferriage or tavern bills will please call and settle. As I have sold my ferry and shall close my tavern with the present month, I must bring things straight.
H. M. Knighton

In 1847, Knighton moved down the river to his town-site, where he and his wife lived in a log cabin. There, his first child, S. C. Knighton, was born. Knighton decided to call his town "Plymouth," the name being suggested by a conspicuous rock which brought to mind another pioneering adventure two centuries earlier. The site had previously been called "Cazeno," after the name of an Indian chief who lived there. Chief Ca-Sa-No became a friend of Hudson's Bay Company, whose agents wooed him with gifts. The chief was especially happy when the Company gave him the duty to fire a salute whenever one of the Company's vessels came in sight bound up the river to Fort Vancouver.

For the first two years, Knighton made few improvements at Plymouth. In October 1847, J. Q. Thornton visited it, on a trip down the river, and was able to report only that the site "has a fine natural wharf." In June 1848, Reverend G. H. Atkinson came to Oregon, and, on the way up the Columbia River, the ship he was aboard anchored briefly off Plymouth. He recorded in his diary that "the magnificent cones of Mts. St. Helens, Rainier, and Hood are all seen at once from Plymouth. Plymouth is finely located, but only one or two persons living there yet." He added that Mr. Knighton came out in a boat to board the ship for a visit, and he described Knighton as "a fine looking man."

In 1850, more active development began at the town-site, which people along the river persisted in calling "Knighton," despite its founder's desire for the anonymity of an impersonal historical reference. In the spring of 1850, the *Spectator*, reflecting popular usage, said "Knighton" was to be one of the stops on the river mail route then being set up. However, when the post office was officially established there, in April 1850, it was under the formal name "Plymouth," with Captain Knighton as postmaster. "Plymouth," which followed by two months the post office created at Milwaukie, was the Territory's thirteenth.

Also in 1850, Knighton built a much more substantial and impressive house for himself. For its exterior and the interior woodwork, he used smooth lumber, a cargo of which was brought round the Horn from New England in 1850. For the house's foundation and framing, he used rough lumber from the sawmill at nearby Milton, which did not have a planer. The house is still standing, and in use as a residence, though it has been moved from its original location. The fact that, built in 1850, this house was one of the first four houses at Plymouth indicates how little development there had been at Knighton's townsite up to that time.

In 1850, Knighton was joined in his townsite venture by William H. Tappan, who had come across the plains in 1849 with the Mounted Rifle Regiment that was part of the new U.S. Army garrison at Fort Vancouver. Tappan was attached to the regiment as a "Special Artist" for the government. He was a man of unusual talents. Presumably an accomplished horseman—certainly an experienced one—he also understood surveying and was an engraver and painter. In 1854, he designed and engraved the seal of Washington Territory, after Washington had been established as a political unit separate from Oregon. An oil painting by him, depicting a scene at The Dalles Methodist Mission, hangs in the Oregon Historical Society's building in Portland. The painting is a useful documentation of the appearance of the Mission in those pre-photography days. Tappan, who was 30 years old, surveyed Knighton's townsite in 1850, laying out streets and lots for its development.

In November 1850, the name of the post office was officially changed from "Plymouth," which had not caught on, to "St. Helen." At that time, Tappan replaced Knighton as post master. The new name was in recognition of the mountain so spectacularly visible from the townsite. The mountain itself was one of the first physical features in the Oregon Country to be named by a European. The name was bestowed upon the mountain by Captain George Vancouver in 1792. At the time, Vancouver was at sea, aboard his ship *Discovery*, off the mouth of the Columbia River. But from there, 100 miles distant, the 9700-foot snowy cone was plainly visible, seen directly up the Columbia River which cuts a path through the intervening hills. Vancouver, in his Journal for October 20, 1792, described his view of the mountain, and added: "This I have distinguished by the name of Mount St. Helens, in honor of his Britannic Majesty's ambassador at the Court of Madrid."

Vancouver's selection of the moutain's namesake was particularly apt. A diplomatist, William Fitzherbert, had been sent, as Ambassador Extraordinary, from Britain to Madrid in 1790, to negotiate a treaty with Spain regarding the use of harbors on the Northwest Coast of America. As a reward for his peaceful settlement of the dispute between Britain and Spain about the "Oregon Coast," Fitzherbert was elevated to the Peerage, receiving the title "Baron Saint Helens."[14] It was, furthermore, as a result of this successful diplomacy that Captain Vancouver himself had been sent out, in the *Discovery*, to the Northwest Coast.

In naming his townsite after the mountain, Knighton initially erred, calling it "St. Helen," without the final "s." However the mountain was properly labeled on most maps, and custom and usage added the "s" to the townsite, too. In 1913, the post office was officially changed to "St. Helens."

Now, with the townsite given an inspiring name, platted in saleable town lots, and with a partner helping Knighton, St. Helens began to see some action. The *Spectator* took note of the stirrings at the downstream townsite with this comment about St. Helens:

> A bountiful supply of building material [the editor was referring simply to the great virgin forest at the townsite's back door] is at hand to build a large town. The proprietors are said to be men of the most liberal enterprise, and well adapted to building up and settling a new country.

In their coming challenge to Portland, the St. Helens proprietors had allies at Milton, a neighboring townsite located about 1½ miles upstream from St. Helens.

Milton. This townsite was at the mouth of Scappoose Bay, a little inlet opposite the downstream end of Sauvie Island. It was on a land claim selected by Captain Nathaniel Crosby, Jr., about 1846. Crosby had come to Oregon as Captain of the *Toulon*, which arrived at Portland, from New York, in October 1845. He engaged, with the *Toulon*, in trade between the Columbia River and Hawaii and California for about four years, returning to his home at Portland about every two months. In 1847, he had built, at Portland, a frame house which was one of the most impressive in Oregon at the time. During 1849-50, he made a small fortune transporting passengers and freight from Oregon to the California gold fields.

Crosby was born in Maine, and was a member of a prominent seafaring family. Two brothers, Clanrick and Alfred, later came round to Oregon to join Nathaniel. Clanrick arrived at Portland in 1850 as master of the brig *Grecian*, from New York. He brought his wife and three children aboard his vessel, and became one of the early residents on Puget Sound, where he established a shipping business. Alfred settled at Astoria in 1850 and was a Columbia River bar pilot for many years.

It was not until the spring of 1850 that Captain Nathaniel Crosby, Jr. began actively to promote his townsite. Prior to that, however, an important development had already been made there. It was a sawmill, built in 1848 by Joseph Cunningham for T. H. Hunsaker. The mill was powered by the water of what later came to be called Milton Creek, after the townsite at its mouth. Hunsaker found an immediate market for his lumber in California, at prices that gave him a worthwhile profit. But after only about a year at the millsite, Hunsaker sold his mill, because there was no school anywhere near there for his children. He moved to Oregon City, and the mill was acquired by Francis Perry and Posey Williams. In 1851, that partnership was dissolved, Perry built a new sawmill two miles farther up Milton Creek, and the Hunsaker mill was taken over by a group of ship captains (Captains Pope, Williams, Drew, and Menzies).[10] Later, principal ownership of the sawmill was acquired by Thomas H. Smith, who had teamed up with Crosby to develop Milton as a town.

"Crosby & Smith," as the Milton team was known, had their offices in Portland up to the summer of 1850. There, they operated as shipping agents, importers, and merchants. Milton, as a town, still existed only on the drawing-boards of their imaginations. The name they chose for the townsite was a tribute to the sawmill already there ("Mill-town") rather than to the great English poet.

In March 1850, Crosby was captain of the bark *Louisiana* on a trip to San Francisco. The *Louisiana* was one of the vessels in Lot Whitcomb's "Milwaukie Line," thus indicating some collaboration between Portland's upstream and downstream enemies. On its trips to California, the *Louisiana* was taking lumber from both the Milwaukie and Milton sawmills. A month later, when the *Louisiana* was back with a cargo of merchandise for Crosby & Smith, they advertised their new stores in the *Spectator*:

JUST RECEIVED

NOW LANDING, per bark *Louisiana*, from San Francisco, and for sale by Crosby & Smith:

A large and general assortment of ready-made clothing.

American and Spanish saddles; black leather and russet bridles; martingales, girths.

Crosby & Smith,
April 1850   Portland

A few days after the *Louisiana's* return, the *Grecian* arrived at Portland from New York, under the command of Captain Clanrick Crosby, with more merchandise for Crosby & Smith. In the *Spectator* of May 2, 1850, Crosby & Smith placed a large advertisement, listing the new goods for sale, and again they indicated their location at Portland, with no mention yet of Milton. However, they were even then preparing the first round to be fired in their battle with Portland, which took the form of an advertisement in the *Spectator* of May 16, 1850:

TOWN OF MILTON

IS SITUATED on the lower branch of the Willamette River, just above its junction with the Columbia. The advantages of its location speak for themselves. All we ask is for our friends to call and see the place.

For Particulars, apply to

Crosby & Smith
Portland and Milton

By August 1850, Crosby & Smith had established their offices at Milton, and Captain Crosby was trying to sell his house in Portland. These two advertisements appeared in the *Spectator* beginning in August 1850:

Nath'l Crosby, Jr.   Thomas H. Smith
CROSBY & SMITH
General Merchandise & Commission
Merchants
M I L T O N , O R E G O N

FOR SALE

OUR entire block, consisting of 8 lots in Portland, together with my dwelling house and the outhouses situated upon the premises. The dwelling house is universally acknowledged to the the finest specimen of architecture in this Territory. Apply to

Nath'l Crosby, Jr.
Portland

In October 1850, Crosby & Smith placed in the *Spectator* an advertisement, in the form of an open letter, which gave a glowing description of Milton and also showed the ways in which they planned to promote their townsite:

TO IMMIGRANTS AND OTHERS

THE undersigned, proprietors of the town of Milton, being desirous to have improvements progress rapidly, propose that they will give to every head of a family 2 town lots and to every single man one town lot, who will become an actual settler in said town within 6 months and build a house upon the same; in addition to which we will sell building materials to those that accept this proposition and allow them a reasonable length of time to pay for them in.

To anyone that will build a good Grist Mill, we will give a mill site together with land sufficient for the purposes of a grist mill.

This town is handsomely located upon the lower branch of the Willamette River, just far enough above its junction with the Columbia to render it an excellent harbor.

Two mountain streams run, one on each side of the town, affording water power sufficient to manufacture 50,000 feet of lumber per day—upon one of which three sawmills are now underway.

Although this town has been laid out but a few months, it has already made much progress in point of improvement and commerce, and bids fair soon to become the most important one in the Territory.

To those desirous of taking up land claims, we would state that we are surrounded by as beautiful and fertile a section of country as Oregon can boast of, including the Scappoose plains, Sauvie's Island, the rich and extensive Prairies lately explored upon the Catlapoodle (or Lewis) river, and the fine land in the immediate vicinity of the town.

Crosby & Smith

NB. We can give permanent employment to quite a number of hands during the winter.

Dryer, in the *Oregonian* in December 1850, wrote the following description of this latest challenger of Portland:

The town of Milton, one mile and a half above St. Helens, is fast improving, and may look forward

with confidence to its future importance. It is well
situated for a town, and surrounded by the finest
agricultural country in Oregon, which is fast settling. We are told that the flats, or bottom land,
which occasionally overflows, are of great extent
and produce abundant grass for the grazing of im-
mense flocks and herds.

As it turned out, the complacent confidence of Crosby
& Smith, and of Editor Dryer, in Milton's future was ill-
founded. About a decade after its somewhat vainglorious
conception, Milton was washed away. Its promoters had
not taken into account the floods which swept down the
rivers every few years. In two floods, one on the Willamette in the winter of 1861-62 and and other on the Columbia in May-June 1862, the few buildings at Milton
were all carried off and never rebuilt. Even before that,
the townsite had failed commercially. But from 1850 to
1853, Crosby & Smith, working with Knighton and Tappan at St. Helens, gave the Portlanders some stimulating
competition.

17. THREATS OF ROADS AND RAILROADS

WHILE GROWTH was beginning at the rival
sites downstream, Portland was also progressing.
During 1851, several stores and three churches were
built at "Little Stump-Town." Early in 1851, Stephen
Coffin and Daniel Lownsdale built the first hotel in Portland that had any pretensions to matching those in "the
States." Associated with the Portland townsite proprie-

tors was the hotelkeeper, McKnight, who announced his
new hotel with this advertisement in the *Spectator*:

COLUMBIAN
CORNER OF
FRONT AND WASHINGTON STREETS
PORTLAND, O.T.

THE undersigned would inform the Public that
he has opened a new Hotel, and having had
many years' experience as a Hotel Keeper, he flat-
ters himself that with the proper facilities within his
reach, the COLUMBIAN will be acceptable to all
who may desire a quiet retreat. The table will be
supplied with all the luxuries and substantials which
the market affords—his bar with the choicest wines
and liquors.

ORLANDO McKNIGHT

May 22, 1851

In the following issue, May 29th, Editor Schnebly of
the *Spectator* inserted a "news item" that was even better advertising:

> The Columbian—We quartered at the Columbian
> Hotel, Portland, during our stay a few days since.
> For once, since we have been in the Territory, were
> we forcibly reminded of the mode of hotel keeping
> such as is to be met with in Baltimore, New York,
> and St. Louis. It may be truly said that there is one
> place in Oregon where the comforts of civilized life
> may be enjoyed.

The editor of the *Statesman*, visiting Portland at this
time, reported that "the sound of the hammer greets you
on every side." In September 1851, Coffin laid a brick
pavement in front of a new building he was erecting, the
first such pavement in Oregon.

However, "Little Stump-Town" still had its problems.
A visitor to Portland in 1851 was shocked at the lack of

warehouse space, noting that along the riverbank were "stoves, iron, ploughs, harrows, everything lying on the banks uncovered—not store-room enough for them." Another difficulty was described by the editor of the *Spectator*, after a visit to Portland in 1851:

> We were not able to penetrate the town to any distance an account of the vast quantities of mud and water that lay in our course. We screwed up our courage to a point sufficient to wade through and wend our way to the printing office, in hopes to grasp Bro. Dryer by the hand. In this we were disappointed. We were informed he had gone out to rusticate—he had gone to Vancouver.

Another visitor wrote that "The streets of Portland are just mud and water, mixed up into a very good batter." And, of course, there were still the stumps, which, even whitewashed, could be treacherous obstacles in the unilluminated dark of night. On one occasion, after an evening of conviviality, it was reported that a Prominent Portlander—out of respect, we shall withhold his name, which is not material—was colliding with the stumps as he walked down the street, flailing them with his stick like Don Quixote fighting windmills.

This was the Portland now being challenged by the St. Helens-Milton combine. As the battle got underway, each side had certain advantages. Portland's development had commenced earlier: its population early in 1850 was about 300, increasing to about 900 in 1851, while St. Helens and Milton had only a few houses. Portland in 1850 had a wharf, warehouse, steam sawmill, tannery, and blacksmith shop, while the only industrial development the rivals could boast in 1850 was their sawmill. Portland also had the weekly *Oregonian* beginning in December 1850 and the weekly *Times* beginning in June 1851. There was no newspaper at the downstream townsites, and Knighton and Crosby had, with chagrin, to place their promotional advertising in the Portland papers. Portland had the further advantage of being closer to the Territorial Capital, which was at Oregon City till 1853 and then at Salem. Portland was also closer to the agricultural regions in the Willamette Valley above Oregon City, where rich prairies were attracting many of the new settlers.

On the other hand, St. Helens was more accessible to shipping. The *Spectator*, in March 1851, commenting on the beautiful location of Knighton's townsite, stated:

> One thing that gives St. Helens importance as a site is that vessels of any size that can cross the bar at the mouth of the Columbia have no obstacles in the way of making that point.

As for Portland, most vessels could reach it without too much difficulty during most seasons of the year. But there were two bars in the river below Portland that caused problems when the water was low. About a mile up the Willamette from its mouth was Post Office Bar. The other bar was at Swan Island.

Portland fought two separate battles with St. Helens-Milton. The two battles reflected the two facets of the fundamental issue at stake: to attract wagons loaded with produce to a point where they could meet ocean-going ships. One battle was fought over the wagons; the other battle was for the ships. Getting the wagons meant competing to provide the best road over the hills to the farms of the Tualatin Valley. Getting the ships involved not only the enterprise of the townsite proprietors but also the question whether the natural channel to Port-

land was adequate for steamships. The battle for the
wagons was fought first.

The importance of good access to the hinterland was
fully appreciated by the early townsite proprietors. They
understood that adequate port facilities are not enough
in themselves to make a great port; there must be a
market for imports and there must be cargo for the ships
to take away. One of the first projects Lovejoy and
Pettygrove had begun, in their strategy to develop the
Portland townsite, was a road over the hills to the Tualatin Valley. They each contributed $100 and hired a
surveyor, Thomas Brown, to find a suitable route. Lovejoy shortly thereafter sold his interest in Portland, and
the road was opened up by Pettygrove. It was in use by
1846. It was simply a pair of ruts winding through the
forest. The route went westward from the head of Washington Street, crossed Tanner Creek near Lownsdale's
tannery, ascended the hill through present Washington
Park, and then followed the ravine in which Burnside
and Barnes Roads now run. It was 12 tortuous miles by
this route from Portland's waterfront to the Tualatin Valley. However, difficult though this road was, it was adequate to draw to Portland some of the farmers' trade
that had previously gone to Oregon City. A description
of what travel was like on the "Pettygrove Road" is contained in a diary of Mrs. Elisabeth Geer, a pioneer settler
in "Yam Hill" County, who travelled over it in February
1848. She and her family came to Oregon in a wagon
pulled by oxen, but they all had to walk and help the
oxen from Portland to the Tualatin Plains because the
wagon was in mud up to its wheel hubs. There was no
surfacing on the oozy forest bed, and they trudged only
nine miles that first day, having started at sunrise.

The proprietors of both Linnton and Milwaukie, meanwhile, had been building roads to tap the Tualatin business, and, though both of those rival routes were long and difficult, the Portlanders felt compelled to improve access to their townsite. In 1849, they opened a better route. The new route was selected by Lownsdale. It followed Tanner Creek from the head of Jefferson Street to the summit at present-day Sylvan. This was the same ravine used by today's "Canyon Road." The new route was shorter than Pettygrove's and also had an easier grade. But the roadway of the "Lownsdale Road" was no better than that of the "Pettygrove Road." It had no surfacing, was full of stumps, and in wet weather was almost impassable.

There were many complaints from the Tualatin farmers about the condition of the roads to Portland. But the Portland Trio, busy with other concerns, did nothing about it until competition forced them to act. Captains Knighton and Crosby, well acquainted with the Lower Willamette areas, knew just where Portland's weakness lay. Their strategy in this first phase of the battle was indicated by an advertisement in the *Spectator* in May 1850:

> 50 LABORERS WANTED to Complete the road from Milton to the Tualatin Plains. Apply to
> Crosby & Smith
> Portland & Milton

The Milton proprietors, at that time, still had their Portland office, which they closed later that year to commit themselves totally to Milton. And, though the advertisement did not say so, their allies at St. Helens were working closely with them on the road project.

During the summer of 1850, the new road was completed, and the *Spectator* in August announced:

> We are informed that the enterprising proprietors of Milton and St. Helens have just completed construction of a new road from those towns to Tualatin Plains.

This road was, according to Captain Crosby, "the easiest, shortest, and best" road from the Plains to the river. Their road took advantage of a low cleft in the hills, used today by Cornelius Pass Road, which required a less sinuous route than the Pettygrove or Lownsdale Roads. The new road was, despite the forgiveable eulogy by Captain Crosby—perhaps he was speaking in terms of travel time rather than distance—somewhat longer than the road to Portland. It was about 30 miles from Hillsboro, in the heart of the Tualatin Valley, to St. Helens, compared with about 20 miles to the Portland waterfront. But, with its easier grade, the new road was a challenge the Portland Trio had to meet.

To find a way to parry their rivals' thrust was not, however, easy; the Canyon Road route already represented the best one nature had provided for Portland. Then Chapman came up with a revolutionary idea: a Railroad! It was a grandiose ploy. The Portlanders announced they would build a railroad from Portland to Lafayette, in "Yam Hill" County. Chapman was its principal promoter, but other Portland capitalists joined the venture. The "Portland & Valley Railroad Company" was incorporated, with capital stock of $500,000. Portlanders subscribed to about $100,000 of the stock, and farmers and merchants along the proposed right-of-way were invited to subscribe to the rest. A "subscription" to such "stock," in those days, represented not an actual purchase for cash, but rather a promise to contribute cash, up to the amount subscribed, when and if called upon to do so. In the case of Portland's railroad, the company never began work nor collected any money from those who had subscribed to the stock. Chapman and his colleagues were more than a decade ahead of their time; development in the Willamette Valley had not yet become dense enough to support profitably the costly investment required for railroad construction and equipment.

However, Portland's railroad proposition did create a stir at the rival townsites downstream. The quick riposte by Knighton, Crosby, and their partners was announced in a large advertisement in the *Spectator*, beginning in November 1850 and continuing through the winter:

R A I L   R O A D
From MILTON and ST. HELENS to LA FAYETTE
Brilliant Chance for Investment!
Work Can Be Completed in 12 Months.
The subscription books are now open.
Crosby & Smith
Milton
W. H. Tappan
St. Helens

NB. The terminus of this road should be at a point that can be reached with safety by large vessels at any season.

The note at the bottom of the advertisement was a pointed jibe at Portland's railroad proposal, implying that the river channel to Portland was inadequate.

The railroad from Lafayette from St. Helens-Milton, like that from Portland, remained only on paper. However, the downstream townsites' new wagon road over the hills to the Tualatin Plains was on the ground, a

viable challenge that Portland had to meet. The proprietors of Portland wistfully turned from their railroad
dream to more prosaic and practical responses: they removed the most offending stumps from Canyon Road
and put "corduroy" (logs laid side by side) in the larger
mud-holes. But something better was needed, and the
Portlanders decided to surface Canyon Road with
planks. Thus was born The Great Plank Road.

18. THE GREAT PLANK ROAD

IN 1851, the Portland & Valley Plank Road Company
was granted a charter by the Territorial Legislature.
This was the first plank road venture in the Oregon
Country. Stock in the company was sold throughout the
Willamette Valley beginning that March. Editor Dryer
lent his support with an article in the *Oregonian* hailing
"The First Plank Road," which he began with this flour-
ish:

> Among the improvements of the age, that of the
> Plank Road deserves particular notice. It allures the
> settler to redeem lands hitherto desolate, and bene-
> fits the farmer in carrying his products to markets.

On July 30, 1851, the stockholders met at Lafayette
to elect officers and make plans for construction of the
road. Lafayette was chosen for the meeting place, just
as it had been named as terminus in the two railroad
schemes, because it was at that time the principal town
in one of the most populous farming areas in the Willamette Valley. Lafayette had been founded in 1847 and

could be reached by small riverboats during months when the Yamhill River was high. It was the terminus of the first steamboat service on the upper Willamette, performed by a little sidewheeler called "Hoosier No. 1." That steamboat had been transported up over "The Falls" in 1851 and began operating between Lafayette, Champoeg, and a landing just above "The Falls" called Canemah. Lafayette was described in a letter written from there in 1851 by an early settler as "the third town in importance in the Territory [presumably after Portland and Oregon City], surrounded by decidedly the richest, healthiest, and most populous country in the Territory." However, later development passed Lafayette by, and today it has about the same population, and much less importance, than it had in the 1850s.

At the Lafayette meeting July 30, 1851, plans were made to complete 10 miles of planked road by November 1st. It was an ambitious and, as it turned out, fantastic commitment. Portland's energetic Stephen Coffin was given the contract for laying the planks. By September, 80 men were at work on the road. Each settler in Portland was asked to contribute two days of work to the project, or to pay someone else to do the work for him. The planks were sawed at Portland's Abrams & Reed steam sawmill.

To construct a plank road, two large logs were first laid lengthwise along the roadbed. These "stringers" were parallel and about as far apart as the length of the planks to be laid across them. Then the planks were laid crosswise, like the ties on a railroad, only, of course, edge to edge, making a sort of plank floor. On flat terrain, such roadways could be reasonably permanent, if the roadbed was properly prepared, but on steep grades,

they tended to wash away. Also, on inclines, it was difficult footing for horses.

By the end of September 1851, work had progressed
sufficiently to permit laying the first plank. Since publicity and promotion were among the benefits Portland's
city fathers hoped to derive from the road, an elaborate
ceremony was planned to celebrate the event. Today, a
bronze plaque on a rock in the Park Blocks between the
Art Museum and the Oregon Historical Society's building commemorates the occasion. On Saturday, September 27, 1851, at 10 A.M., a crowd of spectators assembled
for the festivities. Orators of the day included Editor
Dryer, Chapman, and Stark. When the first, the cere-
monial, plank was laid, Colonel William N. King, superintendent of the Plank Road Co., placed beneath it "a
gold coin bearing the American Eagle" wrapped in a
copy of the program printed for the occasion. As a jour-
nalist of the day expressed it, "The act was accompanied
with appropriate remarks." One of the speakers observed
that "This is the commencement of an era of commercial
prosperity, which will continue to increase until the iron
horse takes the place of the plank road."

After the speeches, a "spacious table" was provided,
set upon the newly-laid planks, and "all partook of the
refreshments." Editor Waterman, in his account of the
event, noted that "Among the dainties of the table, we
noticed a large and well-roasted ox." He added, "The
ladies honored the festival with their presence, a handsome cavalcade being conducted over the new road,
as a sort of trial trip we suppose."

By this time, the roadway had been surveyed to the
summit of the hill, near present-day Sylvan, and orders
were given to continue the survey on from there to

"Hillsborough." But, despite the burst of enthusiasm on the day of the celebration, work on the planking of the road languished, for lack of funds. On November 11, 1851, a meeting of the stockholders was called to devise ways of going on with the work. Progress had halted because stockholders had not responded promptly to calls for the money which they had, by their stock subscriptions, agreed to supply. The total amount of stock subscribed had been $40,800. At the November meeting, company officials reported that only $2905 had been collected from stockholders, but contracts had been let which totalled $11,000.

The partially completed road was badly damaged by rains during the winter of 1851-52, and there was some public criticism of the company. Editor Dryer, in his issue of January 10, 1852, attacked Colonel King, the Plank Road Superintendent, for incompetence. King, a Democrat politician allied with upstate partisan interests, was a frequent target of the Whig editor's displeasure. On this occasion, Dryer wrote:

> We learn that the late rains have seriously injured the work which has been done on the Plank Road, in many places entirely destroying it. Indeed, nothing else could have been expected, as the work was under the superintendence of men entirely unacquainted with the business of building plank roads. A large amount of money is said to have been foolishly expended by those having the work in charge. It is fully time the stockholders should awake and select a *new* and *competent* board of directors, who will push forward the work in a proper manner.

A few days after that editorial blast, the company secretary issued a defensively-toned statement, reviewing the difficulties but asserting that the road "is now the very

best route to reach the plains." A committee of stockholders appointed to examine the road reported in
March 1852, "There is a lack of culverts under the road,
and in consequence of this neglect, the road has been
considerably damaged this past winter."

While the road, in the planked surface originally envisioned, was not completed, a good roadbed had been
prepared for a distance of six miles westward from Portland, and part of it at the lower end, up the canyon from
Jefferson Street, had been planked. The Great Plank
Road was just wide enough for one wagon, and "turn-
outs" were provided so wagons could pass. The total
amount spent by the company by April 1852, when its
efforts ceased, was $14,593. There was a substantial
deficit, since only $6,026 in cash had been collected from
subscribers to the stock.

During the next few years, further improvements were
made. But even though The Great Plank Road, as it was
in 1852, left much to be desired, it was a shorter and now
a better route than St. Helens could offer. Portland, thus,
was "one up" in the battle with the downstream rivals,
and during 1852 rapidly expanded its trade. Now, other
people besides Portland's proprietors began to acknowl-
edge "Little Stump-Town's" growing pre-eminence.
One, for example, was a lawyer named David Logan,
who in November 1850 was living at Lafayette. At that
time, he wrote in a letter to relatives "back East": "I am
living at this place and shall remain there until the point
shall be discovered where the great city of the Pacific is
to be, and to that place I shall go." By February 1852,
Logan had decided that the future lay with Portland, to
which he had moved. In a letter written at that time, he
described Portland as "improving fast. We have seven

steam riverboats leaving this place daily, some as fine as any on the Mississippi. From 10 to 20 sea vessels arrive weekly from California, Chile, Sandwich Islands, China, Australia, etc. We export lumber, flour, oats, potatoes, hogs, beef, etc. to all these countries."[11]

But Captains Knighton and Crosby were not ready to surrender. Perhaps most ocean vessels were then coming to Portland. But the Captains had the vision to look ahead to the day when the larger steamships would replace the relatively small sailing vessels. So there remained another issue which had not yet been resolved: was Portland's river channel really adequate for steamships? Or would St. Helens be the terminus of the ocean steamers, with Portland being served by barges and riverboats coming up from St. Helens?

19. THE BATTLE FOR THE STEAMSHIP LINE

AFTER OPENING THEIR ROAD to Tualatin Plains in 1850, the downstream rivals, demonstrating that "liberal enterprise" the newspaper editors had attributed to them, turned to other schemes to promote their townsites. One of the first events to focus attention on St. Helens and its neighboring communities was a Gala Horse Race Meet, in September 1850. Tappan, late of the "Mounted Rifles," helped organize it. The advertisement for the event, in the *Spectator*, showed that another asset of the St. Helens proprietors was a sense of humor:

THE FALL RACES

Over the Scappoose Course

will commence the 24th of September and continue
for 5 days:

First day, a four-mile race................Entrance,		$100
2nd day, a three-mile race.................	"	$25
3rd day, mile heats, a sweepstake for the best two in three........................	"	$25
4th day, a single heat of one mile....	"	$25
5th day, a slow race for one mile, to be run by mules, the hindmost mule to take the purse...................	"	$1

To conclude with a foot race between two cele-
brated pedestrians.

A brass band has been engaged for the occasion,
and booths will be fitted up for refreshments.

All communications should be addressed to

Wm. H. Tappan
ST. HELENS

During 1850, Knighton, while laying plans to develop
his townsite, was also captain of the bark *Eliza*, sailing
between St. Helens and California. He was hauling lumber from the Milton sawmill to San Francisco, and bringing up merchandise to sell at his store at St. Helens. In
these ventures he was able to make good profits, which
provided capital to invest in his townsite. For example,
in March 1850, he took a cargo of 79,000 board feet of
lumber to San Francisco, charging freight of $70 per
thousand feet, or about $5500 for the one-way voyage,
a handsome sum in 1850. The freight was billed to the
buyer in San Francisco, who also paid enough for the
lumber itself to give the Milton sawmill proprietors an
inspiring profit.

On a voyage in the fall of 1850, Knighton was in San
Francisco, picking up merchandise for his return trip,
when he received a letter from his colleague at Milton,
giving him advice about market conditions at home:

"Relative to bringing up goods, I will say that our market is already much overstocked, and money is becoming exceedingly scarce. Good cigars, good liquors, carpenters' tools, broad and felling axes, nails are in good demand and would sell well.

"Milton and St. Helens are going ahead with a rush. Your family are all well. Hoping to see you soon, I remain,

Yours truly,
Thomas H. Smith"

After that trip, Knighton left the voyages to California to other captains, remained at St. Helens, and concentrated on its development. In February 1851, he placed an advertisement in the *Oregonian*, announcing that he and Tappan were "Dealers in General Merchandise at St. Helens."

As a former hotel-keeper at Oregon City, Knighton appreciated the necessity of having a good hotel at St. Helens. With his help, a hotel was built, and the following advertisement began to appear in the newspapers in March 1851:

A NEW AND SPLENDID HOTEL has just been completed at St. Helens, under the management and direction of the undersigned, who will spare no pains to render a sojourn pleasant and agreeable. Their table will be found to contain the best the Market affords. In fine, this will be found a first-class Hotel. Meals at all hours.

CARTLAND & ATWOOD

Portland, in 1851, had three hotels, all using newspaper advertisements in a similarly grandiloquent style. One of them, the Columbian, was more than a match for the St. Helens House. However, the St. Helens House did advance the townsite's competitive position. Shortly after the opening of the new hotel, Editor Schnebly of the *Spectator* made a trip down the river, and wrote of St. Helens:

> Here is located one of the finest hotels in Oregon;
> its accommodations are said to be Number One.
> But St. Helens, like most of the other towns below
> Oregon City, is yet in embryo as respects improve-
> ment.

But Knighton had plans to make improvements. During
1851, he built a warehouse and wharf. Even more significantly, he began talking with the Pacific Mail Steamship Company about the possibility of their putting up
a dock convenient for the largest steamships.

By October 1851, so much progress had been made at
St. Helens that an old pioneer, returning there for a visit,
felt impelled to write a "Letter to the Editor" of the
Spectator:

> Mr. Editor: It may be possible that all your readers
> and particularly the late emigrants do not know
> there is such a place as St. Helens, or if so, they may
> not know that they have a regular organized city,
> marshal, City Fathers, and all; and can boast of hav-
> ing more good substantial buildings in proportion
> to the number than any town in Oregon. On my
> visit to the place after an absence of 12 months, the
> place was so much altered that it was with difficulty
> I found the residence of my old friend the Captain,
> who introduced me to many distinguished citizens
> of the place.

In 1852, the volume of shipping from St. Helens was
second only to that from Portland, among the ports on
the Willamette and Columbia Rivers. During a six-
month period, 18 barks, ships, and schooners took on
their cargos at St. Helens.

Captain Knighton was not the only enterprising promoter at the downstream townsites. Captain Crosby was
also, at this time, beginning a new adventure to add to
the shipping volume of the St. Helens-Milton com-

munity. He had acquired the bark *Louisiana*, which had formerly been in the "Milwaukie Line," and with her he undertook to open trade with China. In 1852, he took the first shipload of spars to the Orient. The tall, straight fir trees near the Milton mill were ideal for making ships' spars, and they found a ready market in Hong Kong. During Crosby's absence, Milton's affairs were in the hands of his partner, Smith. In 1853, Captain Crosby made a second voyage to China, returning to Oregon in November of that year.

As for the service of the Pacific Mail Steamship Company, Portland and St. Helens were, during 1851, on an equal footing. The mail steamship ordinarily visited neither town, but came only to Astoria. In 1850 and once in April 1851, the mail steamship had come up to Portland. But that was before the riverboat *Willamette* was ready to run on the river. When the *Willamette* was put into service, in the spring of 1851, the P.M.S.Co. announced its regular plan of operation with this newspaper advertisement:

> PACIFIC MAIL STEAMSHIP CO.
>
> The new Steamship *Columbia* will ply between San Francisco and Ports in Oregon. It will leave San Francisco on the arrival of the mail steamer from Panama, with the mails for Oregon, touching at Astoria and returning without delay. The Company's new and splendid river steamer *Willamette* will connect with the *Columbia*, taking passengers for St. Helens, Portland, and Oregon City.

By this line, passengers could go from Portland to San Francisco in about a week. The fare was $75 cabin, $45 steerage. Even the steerage fare was more expensive than a first-class trans-Atlantic crossing today, when inflated to 1970 wages and prices. Of course, there were numerous sailing vessels visiting both Portland and St. Helens, and passengers could go to California aboard one of them for much less money, though with a corresponding decrease in the certainty of getting there. A very good passage, by sail, from Astoria to San Francisco, was seven days. Two or three weeks was normal, and sometimes it took a month. The more adventureful voyages could give surviving passengers an engaging topic of conversation. An example of an all-too-frequent sort of entry in the records of the Port of Astoria was this, for January 11, 1852:

> "Schooner Matthew Vasser just in, 28 days from San Francisco. She was short of provisions and water; experienced heavy gales and lost some of her sails."

From the summer of 1851 to January 1852, the P.M.S.Co's. shuttle operation, up-river from Astoria, worked without serious miscarriage, though there were many complaints about irregularity of mail service. Some of the uncertainties and hazards that could interrupt the *Willamette's* river run were described in the diary of a man who made the trip in May 1851, from which these excerpts are paraphrased:

Left Portland 7 A.M. on steamer *Willamette*. A beautiful boat. A good number of passengers. At 9:30 A.M. stopped at Fort Vancouver, took on the mail. At noon arrived at St. Helens for the mail, got aground, and lay until 4 P.M. [when the tide raised the vessel], and then went on down to the Cowlich River, took in several cords of wood. At midnight the boat ran on shore owing to a difficulty with the tiller ropes. We lay there all the next day, working to get her off. The following day, when the tide raised in the morning, she was able to back out. At Astoria, the mail steamer arrived soon after we came to anchor. I went aboard her, took forward cabin passage. At 8 A.M. left Astoria, and crossed the bar. The time passed pleasant. Several sea sick. Kept in sight of land all the way and enjoyed ourselves very well.

In January 1852, however, the *Willamette* had a more serious accident. She ran aground, between Portland and Milwaukie, on the "Ross Island Bar" that had been Whitcomb's downfall. The *Oregonian* of January 17th reported:

> The Steamer *Willamette* is aground about three miles above this city. The water was falling fast, which has removed all hopes of getting the steamer off until a rise takes place in the river. This accident is much to be regretted as it will prevent the *Willamette* from performing her regular trips in the transmission of the mails. The ocean steamer *Columbia* will extend her semi-monthly trips to Portland; therefore, no delays or inconvenience in the transmission of the mail or to passengers will occur.

Under this emergency plan, the P.M.S.Co's ocean steamship *Columbia* proceeded up to Portland with the mail on January 19, 1852 and again on February 8th. A few days after that, the *Willamette* was refloated, and was at Astoria on February 26th to meet the *Columbia* on her next trip. However, the P.M.S.Co. had discovered there might be an advantage in having the *Columbia* terminate its run regularly at one of the ports on the Lower Willamette, rather than at Astoria. The Lower Willamette was the source of nearly all its freight and passenger traffic, and if a large depot could be built at the "head of navigation," the shuttle service of the *Willamette* could be eliminated. The P.M.S.Co. was finding, as Lot Whitcomb had found, that population and industry in Oregon had not yet grown to a size that would permit a large, expense riverboat to operate profitably. And there were now several small steamboats operating on the river that could be hired to bring freight and passengers to a central depot. But where should

that depot be? Company officials had doubts about nav-
igability of the Willamette River at Post Office Bar and
Swan Island Bar during the months of low water. Cap-
tain Knighton had nurtured those doubts. So the com-
pany's choice fell to St. Helens. In February 1852, the
P.M.S.Co. announced that it was moving its principal
Oregon office from Portland, where it had been, to St.
Helens, and that the mail steamship would henceforth
not stop at Astoria but would come up the river to St.
Helens. The *Spectator* of February 24, 1852, reported:

> ☞ A large meeting was recently held at Port-
> land to take into consideration the removal of the
> Mail Steamship Company's head-quarters from that
> place down to St. Helens. It was resolved by the
> citizens of the former place, that they will, for the
> future, in no way patronize the vessels belonging
> to that Company. A large amount of indignation
> was spent at the meeting, which will, no doubt,
> affect but little the determination of the Company,
> which is so much of a monopoly that it generally
> manages its business to suit its own immediate
> interests.

Beginning in April 1852, St. Helens became the mail
steamship's terminus. The P.M.S.Co. was able to make
its move to St. Helens because Knighton, by this time,
had built a warehouse and wharf. But the Company also
announced that it was buying land at St. Helens and
would construct a warehouse of its own and a large
wharf designed specifically for the use of steamboats.

Passengers and freight from Portland were, for the
time being, taken down to St. Helens by the *Willamette*.
This arrangement continued for several months. Then,
in August 1852, the *Willamette* was transferred to California and put on the company's more profitable San
Francisco-Sacramento route. Without the *Willamette* to

provide pick-up service, the company reversed its earlier decision and began to send the mail steamship on up to Portland. The company felt obliged to take such navigational risks as there may have been in order to compete with sailing vessels for the freight and passenger traffic originating at Portland, which continued to provide most of the business on the river. However, St. Helens remained the company's Oregon headquarters and the principal terminus.

One reason the P.M.S.Co. reversed its decision, that the Willamette River was too risky for its steamship, was that the Portland proprietors were making a determined effort to belittle the supposed dangers of Swan Island Bar. In September 1852, the Portland proprietors made a survey of the channel in the Willamette and inserted the following "Letter to the Editor" in the *Oregonian*:

> Sir: The undersigned have this day made thorough examination of the channel over Swan Island Bar, and find 12 feet 3 inches of water in the channel at low tide; so that at high water, there is 15 feet in the channel, the tide rising three feet at Portland. The Willamette River is now at the lowest stage known for many years.
>
> Z. C. Norton
Stephen Coffin
W. W. Chapman
>
> September 17, 1852

Captain Norton was owner of a wharf along Portland's waterfront. As for the depth, even the 12 feet at low tide was quite adequate for the steamship *Columbia*, provided the channel was wide enough and the pilot could stay in it.

Editor Dryer also felt called upon to speak out on the subject of the Swan Island Bar. In the same issue containing the letter from Coffin and his friends, Dryer wrote, in the imperative and forceful style that enlivened nineteenth-century journalism:

> Swan Island Bar—The brig *Francisco* and the bark *I. B. Lunt*, the former drawing 11 feet 3 inches and the latter 10 feet 6 inches, were taken over this bar by the steamer *Lot Whitcomb* on Monday last, at dead low water. This ought to satisfy everybody that the difficulty in crossing Swan Island Bar is only imaginary. Ship masters and pilots assure us that at the lowest stage there is from 12 to 15 feet of water on the bar. Comment is unnecessary—facts settle this question beyond doubt.

Despite these assurances, on one of her first trips up the Willamette River, after the steamship *Columbia* had resumed serving Portland, she ran aground on Swan Island Bar. Dryer reported the incident in his issue of October 9, 1852, but — which was considered proper news-writing in those days — he took care to show the mishap in the most favorable light. His report noted that the *Columbia* had "touched on Swan Island Bar, where she was detained several hours awaiting the rising of the tide. The Willamette River has never been known to be so low as it is at the present time. This, together with the fact that it was the lowest ebb of the tide, will account for the detention."

Dryer's reassuring explanation did not make the *Columbia's* owners comfortable about standing their vessel, however, and they continued to make plans eventually to terminate their run at St. Helens, and provide some local service from there to Portland. Later in October 1852, the *Oregonian* reported:

> There are several important improvements being made in the river towns below. The Pacific Mail

> Steamship Company is building a wharf at St. Hel-
> ens; Mr. Knighton has already erected a fine wharf
> and warehouse there.

Editor Dryer, complacent in his conviction that Portland's dominance was secure, showed no animosity
towards St. Helens, where his newspaper circulated
without local opposition. The *Oregonian* was regularly
carrying Knighton's personal business advertisement, as
an import-export "Commission Agent." However, Dryer
did give himself the pleasure of aiming a retaliatory shot
at St. Helens, in return for the downstream proprietors'
insinuations about Swan Island Bar. He wrote, with
impish innuendo:

> DROWNED — We learn that John Rodgers, a
> worthy citizen of Scappoose plains, was found
> drowned at St. Helens a few days since. It appears
> that almost everyone who accidentally gets into the
> river about St. Helens is drowned. There must be
> some unusual currents, or other causes at that point,
> to occasion this loss of life.

During this interlude, from September 1852 to November 1853, the P.M.S.Co's. steamships came to Portland on almost every trip. Usually, the vessel sent up
from San Francisco was the *Columbia*, though occasionally the smaller *Fremont* was used. The *Columbia* was
generally able to make the trip between San Francisco
and towns on the Lower Willamette in four or five days,
with a two-day turnaround at each end. This meant she
was at St. Helens and Portland about twice a month.
And she arrived with regularity, considering the hazards
and technology of the 1850s.

Despite the appearance that all was well with Portland's steamship connection, the P.M.S.Co. had other
plans. The company was pushing completion of its new

wharf at St. Helens. During the summer of 1853, about
60 men were working on its construction, and living at a
boarding hotel in St. Helens. In October 1853, the *Oregonian* reported:

> We learn that many valuable improvements are going forward at St. Helens. The Pacific Mail Steamship Company have just completed a substantial wharf and store-house. Mr. Knighton has also completed a wharf. Mr. DuRell is now building a large steam saw and grist mill, which will add much to the growing business of the place.

The P.M.S.Co. wharf cost about $40,000, equivalent to
at least ten times that amount if expressed in terms of
1970 prices and wages.

Then, on October 22, 1853, the *Oregonian* published
an announcement that created consternation and dismay
at Portland: the mail steamer would thenceforth terminate at St. Helens. Passengers and freight would be
taken between Portland and St. Helens by the riverboat
Multnomah. And, beginning with her trip of November
12th, the *Columbia*, as threatened, came only as far as
St. Helens. This was the second time the company had
cut off service to Portland. But this time, the move
seemed more deliberate, planned and decisive.

The reaction of Portlanders to this change was described in a letter written at the time by Charles Stevens'
to relatives "back East." He said that "The people in
Portland are very indignant about it, held indignation
meetings, burned the mail agent in effigy, and are intending to get another steamer on the line, and let the
old *Columbia* whistle."

One of the protest meetings evoked Editor Dryer's
wrath, partly because its leader was a Democrat politician who was anathema to the Whig editor. Dryer's

denunciation, which might have been penned with a mixture of ink and vinegar, was in the quaint manner that came to be known among journalists as "the Oregon style." In his editorial, Dryer also explained his reasons for appearing calm, almost indifferent, to Portland's loss of the steamship terminus. He wrote, in November 1853:

SMALL POTATOES

About the smallest affair which has been got up lately in this city by the *Small Potato* agitators was a meeting held at the Canton House, to instruct the Pacific Mail Steamship Company where they should stop the steamer *Columbia*. . . . The smallest of the *small fry* [has] assumed that the future growth, commercial importance, and prosperity of the city of Portland depend entirely upon the fact whether the Steamer *Columbia* stops at St. Helens or comes up to Portland.

This left-handed compliment to the city is in perfect keeping with the bigoted mind of the "Bogtrotter" and his numerous assistants. . . . Any man with the brains of a musquito will not fail to see the utter foolishness of this great cry about the steamer's stopping at St. Helens. If Portland possesses commercial advantages over St. Helens or any other point on the river below, no company can successfully retard its growth. The commercial business will continue, as it has done, to center at this point.

True, it may be a source of some inconvenience, delay, and expense to our merchants in the receipt of their goods—yet as they are not compelled to ship by the *Columbia*, unless they choose, they are not materially injured by the present arrangement.

Portland, we are proud to say, possesses advantages in a commercial point of view superior to any other town in Oregon. Business concentrates here— our merchants and business men possess capital, enterprise, experience, and sagacity equal to those of any other point.

We know that its fortune or prosperity does not depend upon so small a matter as to where the

Company may deem fit to stop their steamer. Let
them go where they please; the city of Portland is
entirely independent of them, or their favors. We
can do far better without their aid, than they can
without ours.

The statement that Portland's merchants were not
compelled to use the *Columbia* was a reminder that
there were many sailing vessels in the trade between
Portland and other ports on the Coast at this time. However, their service was slower, more hazardous, and less
regular than that of the steamship.

20. A NEW STEAMSHIP: VICTORY
FOR PORTLAND

DESPITE DRYER'S sanguine confidence, the decision to terminate the *Columbia* at St. Helens was
a victory for Captain Knighton that the Portland proprietors could hardly ignore. Therefore, as they had done
three years earlier in attracting the steamer *Gold Hunter*,
they let it be known that Portland was ready, willing,
and able to support any steamship that would serve
it. The appeal was heard, and, in response to the invitation, a new steamship came up the river to Portland.
It was the *Peytona*,[12] a side-wheel steamer of 850 tons,
somewhat larger than the P.M.S.Co's. *Columbia*. The
Peytona arrived Christmas Day 1853, and its officers
were feted at holiday celebrations in the joyful city. The
day after the ship's arrival, a banquet was given in honor
of the *Peytona*, as reported in this item in the *Oregonian*:

A welcome was given to Captain Nash and the officers of the Steamship *Peytona*, on Monday evening last, in the way of an oyster supper. T. J. Dryer was called to preside. After the supper was over, toasts, sentiments, and speeches from those present occupied the time until a late hour. The utmost harmony and good feeling prevailing through out, and an earnest assurance given to Captain Nash that the feelings of the community were with him in his enterprise.

Dryer not only presided at the banquet, but also published a special edition of his paper, with a large, black banner headline across the top of the front page, saying:

States and California Edition by the Steamship Peytona

On the day after the banquet, a meeting was held to organize support for the *Peytona* and encourage her captain, James L. Nash, who was also one of her owners, to come regularly to Portland. The *Oregonian*, under the headline "A Meeting of the Merchants of Portland," re-

Stock engraving used by the Oregonian in the 1850s at head of its out-of-state news column. The name of the ship bringing the news was inserted in the banner.

ported that more than 60 firms and businessmen had endorsed the following resolution:

> Whereas, the recent course of the Pacific Mail Steamship Company, in stopping their regular vessels at St. Helens, is antagonistic to the best interests of Portland,
>
> Be it therefore resolved: That we, the merchants and business men of Portland, pledge ourselves to encourage and sustain the steamship *Peytona*, now in port, to continue as a regular packet between this city and San Francisco, by giving her all our freight and influence.

Among those signing the resolution were Stephen Coffin and John H. Couch. Chapman had moved away from Portland, to Southern Oregon, earlier in 1853. And Lownsdale had become estranged from Chapman and Coffin as a result of an involved and bitter argument about land titles. Lownsdale had ceased to play a leading role in Portland's affairs and was not present at the meeting to support the *Peytona*. By this time, Portland's destiny was in the hands of those two New Englanders, Coffin and Couch, and other enterprising men who had by now come to Portland, including two more New Englanders, W. S. Ladd and Capt. George Flanders.

Two weeks later, the *Peytona* was back at Portland, from San Francisco. The *Oregonian* of January 14, 1854 reported, with satisfaction, that "the steamship *Peytona* beat the *Columbia's* time about six hours on her last trip up." That issue of the paper also included this item:

> Steamer *Peytona* — The Steamship *Peytona* left on Tuesday afternoon for San Francisco. She had a large number of passengers and a good freight list. We are positively assured by Captain Nash and the agent, Mr. Goddard, that the *Peytona* will continue to run as a regular packet between this city and

San Francisco. Those persons who may desire to visit California or send freight can rest assured that this Steamer will leave about the 24th of this month.

The hazards of navigation upset Editor Dryer's assurances slightly: the *Peytona* did return, but ice in the Columbia River in February 1854 slowed its progress so much that it required ten days to come from Astoria to Portland. However, the P.M.S.Co. steamer, bound for St. Helens, was in the river at the same time, and also took about ten days from Astoria to St. Helens. On this trip, the *Peytona* brought about 40 passengers to Portland from San Francisco, and took about the same number down, on the return trip. At this time, the following advertisement was appearing in the Territory's newspapers:

> New Steamship for San Francisco
> The New & Elegant Steam - Ship
> **P E Y T O N A**
> 850 Tons Burthen
> Has Commenced running on the route from San Francisco to Portland, touching at Astoria.

The P.M.S.Co., meanwhile, was beginning to feel the pressure. There was not enough freight to be taken to and from St. Helens to fill its steamer. The company had expected to continue to handle Portland's freight by hauling it by riverboat to St. Helens. So, in its issue of February 4, 1854, the *Oregonian* was able to announce a triumph for Portland:

> The Pacific Mail Steamship Company's steamer was advertised in the San Francisco papers for Portland, in place of St. Helens, as heretofore. We infer from this that we are to have two semi-monthly steamships running from Portland to San Francisco.

The editor had to find out this momentous change indirectly, by reading the San Francisco papers, because the company's Oregon representatives, at their St. Helens office, had not yet had the fortitude to come up the river to tell Portlanders about the company's surrender.

A letter, written February 5, 1854 by a Portland resident to friends in the "East," described one of the benefits resulting from the new competition in steamship service:

"The new steamer from New York [the *Peytona*] is now running from San Francisco to Portland, once in two weeks, in opposition to Adams & Co. [the agents at Portland for the P.M.S.Co. line]. The old *Columbia* used to charge $75 for passage in the cabin; the *Peytona* put it down to $60, and now the old *Columbia* only charges $10. It is a very good time for people that wish to travel, yet we, or the people feel like supporting the *Peytona*."

The *Oregonian,* too, continued its support of the *Peytona,* with articles such as this, which appeared in a special edition issued February 15, 1854 to be taken that day by the *Peytona* to California:

The steamship *Peytona* arrived here from San Francisco on Sunday last, having made the quickest run of any other vessel between the two ports. The *Peytona* is THE steamship on the coast, and is fast becoming a great favorite with the public on account of her speed, sea-worthiness, and adaptation to the safety and comfort of the passengers and shippers. She ought to be liberally patronized by Oregonians.

As advertised, the P.M.S.Co's steamship did come up to Portland, arriving February 15, 1854. Thereafter, the mail steamer regularly terminated its trips at Portland. St. Helens became only a stop along the way, and soon even the stop there was eliminated. The company's

costly dock at St. Helens was left to sailing vessels loading lumber. The dock was later destroyed by a fire.

Later in February 1854, another steamer, the *America*,
arrived at Portland from San Francisco. The shipping
community, having heard the Portlanders' invitation, had
become aware that a growing volume of freight and
passenger traffic was available at Portland, and that
there appeared to be no insurmountable navigational
problems in the way of getting there. Now, three steamships were running between Portland and San Francisco;
the victory of Portland over its rivals was complete.

There was some irregularity in the steamship service
to Portland during the ensuing months. The *America*
was tied up, literally and figuratively, by a legal quarrel,
and the *Peytona* was replaced by the *Southerner*, which
was wrecked. But there was no longer any doubt that
Portland was the head of navigation and the future
metropolis of the Oregon Country. It was the final
triumph for the judgment of those who had thrown in
their lot with "Little Stump-Town."

EPILOGUE

THE SUBSEQUENT histories of Portland's two
downstream rival townsites, and of their propri-
tors, have some fateful and tragic elements. By early
1854, the townsite ambitions of the four principal proprietors—Knighton and Tappan, and Crosby and Smith—
had been dashed. Later that year, in December,
Columbia County was organized as a political unit, and

Thomas Smith became County Clerk. It was a prosaic step down from the proprietorship of a townsite proclaimed as "soon to become the most important in the Territory." Smith held the office of County Clerk for several years. He moved from Milton to St. Helens, only about a mile away, which was the County Seat. Since there were no county buildings, the "Court House," when there was county business to perform, was in his home. The Milton townsite was inundated by floods during 1861-62. Its few buildings were washed away and never rebuilt. Today, one looks in vain for so much as a bit of rotted piling to show the location of that ambitious venture. The site, on a small quiet bay, is now inhabited only by waterfowl, though imposing industrial plants are visible at no great distance.

Captain Crosby's interests had been divided between his Milton townsite and his shipping to the Orient. When Milton faded, he devoted his time fully to shipping. In 1854, he undertook a third voyage to China, again as captain of the *Louisiana*. The *Oregonian* announced Crosby's voyage with this item:

> FOR HONG-KONG — Capt. N. Crosby, Jr., long identified with the commercial enterprise of Oregon, will sail for Hong-Kong in the bark *Louisiana*. We understand the brig *Cyclops* is also being loaded, at Puget Sound, by Clanric Crosby, a brother of Capt. Crosby, for the same destination. It is the intention of Capt. Crosby to return by way of Japan, and enter all the ports that are opened to American vessels, with a view of learning the commercial advantages to be derived from a trade between this coast and Japan. We wish Capt. Crosby fair winds, a quick passage, and a safe return.

Crosby made a fourth trip to China in 1855, sailing from Portland. This time, he remained there, opening a shipping agency at Hong Kong to handle that end of the trade he was building up between the Pacific Northwest and the Orient. But, in December 1856, victim of an infectious disease, he died suddenly.

As for St. Helens, it had been built on higher ground than Milton, and survived the floods of 1861-62. Long before that, however, Capt. Knighton and Tappan had sold their interests there. St. Helens remained a small riverfront village, whose population only began to increase slowly several decades later. Tappan moved to Vancouver in 1853. He was a representative, from Clark County, to the first Territorial Legislature for Washington, which met in 1854. He later returned to his native Massachusetts.

Knighton was still at St. Helens in 1854, where he was named among those on a jury list for that year. His occupation was shown as "Merchant." Shortly thereafter, however, he, too, moved to Vancouver. He became a riverboat captain. In 1863, he was captain of the steamboat *Iris*, which was running on the Columbia River. That year, he died, of typhoid fever. The *Oregonian* carried this brief notice:

> DIED, at The Dalles, June 17th, Capt. H. M. Knighton, of Vancouver, W. T., formerly of St. Helens, aged 43. His remains were brought to Vancouver for interment. He leaves a wife and six children.

By a curious coincidence, Portland's two principal rivals, Knighton and Whitcomb, were both—if our deductions concerning Whitcomb's inadequately diagnosed ailment are correct—victims of typhoid fever.

In victory, Portland was magnanimous, if one may

judge from the tone of Editor Dryer, who wrote, towards the end of the battle of the townsites:

> The day has gone for any jealousy or rivalry between this and other trading points on the Willamette. So intimate are their relations, and so closely blended are their interests, that the growth and prosperity of any one of them should be a cause of congratulation to all the others.

Business at the rival townsites downstream dwindled away to the point where those small settlements were served quite adequately by one little side-wheel steamboat making tri-weekly trips from Portland. That riverboat was the *John H. Couch.* The name was appropriate, for Couch, along with Pettygrove and Coffin, had been one of destiny's principal agents in determining the victory of "Little Stump-Town."

FINIS.

NOTES

1. In the 1840s, British naval vessels were distinguished by the royal title "His Britannic Majesty's Ship," or "H.B.M.S." Today, that has been shortened to "His (or Her) Majesty's Ship," or "H.M.S." (See page 15)

2. A log cabin had been built a short distance to the south of what later became the Portland townsite land claim, though within the limits of present-day Portland, in 1842 by William Johnson. (See page 30)

3. A brother of Henderson Luelling, Seth Luelling, who was also a nurseryman and orchardist, came with his family to Oregon in 1850, settling near Milwaukie and adding to the town's enterprise. The family name is sometimes spelled Lewelling. (See page 60)

4. Because the Pacific Mail Steamship Company's ocean-going vessel and a small river steamboat were both called *Columbia,* there has been minor confusion in some accounts of early navigation. For example, it has been stated that the mail steamship went up to Oregon City. The P.M.S. Co. steamship *Columbia* never came farther up the river than Portland, though the riverboat *Columbia* was often at Oregon City. (See pages 82 and 97)

5. Some accounts describe the *Willamette* as propeller-driven. She was originally propeller-driven, when she was running on the East Coast. However, for service on the Columbia and Willamette rivers, she was converted to a side-wheeler. The work was done at Portland during April 1851. (See page 91)

6. The size of the *Lot Whitcomb* in one account is put at 212 tons. I have used 300 tons because that is the figure stated in a newspaper report published in 1850 describing the design of the vessel. Actually, there are several ways of measuring ship tonnage, each giving different results. One of the most frequently used methods of computation is called "Custom House" measure, which is based on the volume, in cubic feet, of the interior of the vessel. In terms of an approximation of that measure, it appears that 300 tons is a reasonable figure for the *Lot Whitcomb.* (See page 96)

7. Some accounts, written long after the event, state that the *Lot Whitcomb* "at first made no stops at Portland," or that the Milwaukie owners "refused to allow their steamboat to stop at Portland." It is a colorful story, but unfortunately it does not appear to be based on fact. She did not make her first trial run till the end of January 1851, and began regular service early in February, at which time newspaper advertisements clearly indicated a regular stop at Portland. In fact, Portland was too well established as a source of

traffic to be ignored by any riverboat, which would have been appreciated by an astute businessman like Captain Whitcomb. The myth might have originated from some incident during a trial run, when the *Lot Whitcomb* may have steamed gaily, even flauntingly, past Portland. (See page 102)

8. I have called it the "Democrat Party" rather than the "Democratic Party" because that was the spelling sometimes used by the press in the 1850s and also as a reminder that it was fundamentally different from the modern Democratic Party. The pre-Civil War "Democrat Party" in Oregon was essentially rural, while the town populations were preponderantly Whig, and later Republican. This is the reverse of the main sources of allegiance to the two parties today. (See page 120)

9. The quotations are from the "Letters of Charles Stevens," reproduced in the Oregon Historical Society *Quarterly,* v. 37. (See pages 123 and 166)

10. Positive identification of the full names of these captains, or their vessels, has not been possible, but they probably were Seth Pope, master of the *Nonpareil;* Posey Williams, master of the *Forrest;* George Drew, master of the *Louisiana;* and James Menzies, master of the *O. C. Raymond.* (See page 138)

11. The quotations are from the "Letters of David Logan," reproduced in the Oregon Historical Society *Quarterly,* v. 44. (See page 155)

12. Some accounts incorrectly spell the name of this steamship as "Peytonia." Confusion arose from the fact that there was at least one other vessel with a similar name: the riverboat or "steam scow" *Peytonia.* (See page 168)

13. "Blue Ruin" was English slang for gin, especially gin of inferior quality. For example, William Hazlitt, in a story called "The Fight" written in the early 1800s, referred to a bellicose man as being "more full of *blue ruin* than of good manners."(See page 20)

14. The Baron's title, "St. Helens," was taken from that of a town in England, near Liverpool. The town itself got that name because it grew up around a parish church dedicated to "Saint Helen," a saint who lived in the third century A.D.(See page 136)

INDEX

A

Abernethy, George: Abernethy & Co., 73, 115, 116; Governor, 21; Store at Oregon City, 20.

Abrams, William P.: Sawmill, 69, 151.

Ainsworth, John C., Captain: 93, 96, 117.

America, steamship: 173.

Atkinson, Rev. G. H.: 134.

B

Baillie, Captain of *Modeste*: 15.

Barlow, Samuel: 120.

Bateau, type of riverboat: 24.

Bell, George: 35.

Berry, William J.: 111.

Black Hawk, riverboat: 115.

Boundary, International, news of settlement: 41.

Brown, Thomas: 32, 146.

Burnett, Peter: 127-9.

Burns, Hugh: Arrives Oregon City 1842, 22; Founds Multnomah City, 27.

Bush, Asahel: 99.

C

California, steamship: 84.

Campbell, Samuel: 109.

Capital, finance: 86.

Carolina, steamship: 83, 84, 86, 94, 95.

Carter, William: 73, 96, 118-9.

Caruthers, Finice: 37.

Cathlamet: 102.

Champoeg: 19.

Chapman, William W.: Biography, 65; Buys Portland interest, 65; Agent for *Gold Hunter*, 88; Railroad promotion, 148; Surveys river depth, 163.

Chenamus, brig: 21-2, 29, 38.

Clackamas Rapids: 21, 27-8.

Coal, near Cowlitz River: 102-3.

Coburn, James, Capt.: 78.

Coffin, Stephen: Biography, 64, 80; Buys Portland interest, 64; Builds

steamship, 82; Buys *Gold Hunter*, 89; Plank Road, 151; Steam sawmill, 69; Surveys river depth, 163; Cited, 170.

Columbia, H.B.Co. bark: 45.

Columbia, riverboat: 97-8.

Columbia, steamship: 82-3, 90.

Columbia City: 16.

Commodore Stockton, brig: 45.

Constance, British ship: 48.

Couch, Capt. John H.: First trip to Oregon 1840, 19; trip to Oregon 1842, 21; Opens Oregon City store, 21-2; Anchors at Portland, 29-30; Calls Portland "head of navigation," 38, 107-8; trip to Oregon 1844, 38; Leading citizen of Oregon City, 39; Claim at Portland, 39, 170.

Cowlitz: 102.

Crosby, Capt. Alfred, 138.

Crosby, Capt. Clanrick: 138-9.

Crosby, Capt. Nathaniel, Jr.: Captain of *Toulon*, 33, 41; House at Portland, 42-3, 140; Calls Portland "head of navigation," 111; At Milton, 127, 137-41; Trade to Orient, 158-9, 174-5.

Cunningham, Joseph: 138.

D

Dennison, A. P.: 87.

Desdemona, bark: 73, 96.

Donation Land Claim Law: 16.

Dryad, brig: 6.

Dryer, Thomas J.: 76-8, 87, 105, 112, 124, 165, 167.

E

Eagle, riverboat: 115.

Eliza, bark: 156.

F

Fama, bark: 24.

Flanders, Capt. George: 170.

Forrest, brig: 61.

Fort Hall: 9, 22.

Fort Vancouver: 12, 13, 16, 17.

179

Fort Victoria: 13.
Fort William: 10, 11.
Francisco, brig: 164.
Fremont, steamship: 165.

G

Gaines, Gov. John P.: 99, 100, 112.
Geer, Mrs. Elizabeth: 146.
Geer, Ralph: 60.
Gold Hunter, steamship: 82, 84-90.
Gold Rush, effects on Oregon: 49-55.
Goliah, steamship: 91, 103.
Grecian, brig: 138.

H

Hall, D. W.: Captain of *Keoka*, 78, 104.
Hall, T. A.: Captain of *Ocean Bird*, 78, 104; Captain of *Gold Hunter*, 87, 88, 89.
Henry, brig: 45, 49.
Honolulu, schooner: 47-8.
Hoosier No. 1, riverboat: 115, 151.
Hotels: At Oregon City, 58, 131; At Portland, 143; at St. Helens, 157.
Howison, Lt. Neil, U.S.N.: Describes Portland in 1846, 37; Describes Linnton, 128.
Hudson's Bay Co.: Dominates trade, 11; Immigration policy, 13, 16; Warehouses, 55.
Hunsaker, T. H.: 138.
Hunt, H. H.: 82.

I

I. B. Lunt, bark: 164.
Iris, riverboat: 175.
Immigrants, by year: 2.

J

Jennings, Berryman: 94.
John H. Couch, riverboat: 176.
Johns, James: 127, 129-30. .

K

Kamm, Jacob: 92-3, 96.
Kelley, Hall: 4-6.
Kellogg, Joseph: 61, 94, 109.
Keoka, bark: 62, 77, 78, 79, 104.
Kilborn, William K.: Captain of *Henry*, 49, 99; Mayor of Oregon City, 49, 100.
King, Col. William: 50, 152, 153.
Knighton, Capt. Henry M.: 127, 130-7; 175.
Knighton, S. C.: 134.

L

Ladd, W. S.: 170.
Lafayette, town: 150-1; 154.
Lausanne, ship: Brings Methodists in 1840, 20.
Lee, Daniel: Accompanies Jason Lee, 8.
Lee, Jason: Trip to Oregon with Wyeth, 8-9.
Linn City: 27.
Linn, Senator Lewis F.: Free land bill, 16, 127.
Linnton, 127-9.
Logan, David: 154.
Loomis, James: 120.
Lot Whitcomb, steamboat: Machinery purchased, 93, 96; Specifications, 96; Naming, 98-9; Launching, 100-101; Wins race, 103; Sold, 117.
Louisiana, bark: 62, 73, 96, 104, 139, 159.
Lovejoy, A. L.: Arrives Oregon City 1842, 22; Acquires Portland claim, 31; Sells claim to Stark, 33-4.
Lownsdale, Daniel: Arrives Portland 1845, 36; Tannery, 36; Buys Portland claim, 43, 64; Divides tract with Stark, 67; Road to Tualatin, 147.
Luelling, Henderson: Nurseryman at Milwaukie, 60-1, 109.

M

Malaria: 122-3.
Maryland, brig: Reaches Oregon City 1840, 19-20, 28.
Mary Melville, bark: 112.
Massachusetts, U.S.N. steamship: 83.
Matthew Vassar, schooner: 160.
May Dacre, brig: 8, 11.
McCarver, Morton M.: 127-9.
McKnight, Orlando: 143.
McLoughlin, David, in Oregon City store, 25.
McLoughlin, Dr. John: Controls Oregon trade, 4, 12; Moves to Oregon City, 13; Mayor of Oregon City, 25; Toast to Oregon, 46.
McLoughlin House, 25.
Merchantman, schooner: 101.
Methodist missions: 20-1, 135.
Milton, town: 127, 137-42.
Milwaukie: Description, 63, 105-6; Industries, 59, 60, 61; Malaria, 122-3; Navigation, 108-113; Pop-

ulation, 56, 126; Post Office, 63; Sawmill, 59, 114; Shipyards and shipping, 56, 61, 104; Tree nursery, 60.
Milwaukie, schooner: 61.
Modeste, British sloop: 14-15, 37, 132.
Money, supply and types: 54.
Moore, Robert: Pioneer of 1840, 27; Founds Linn City, 27; Promotes water power, 28.
Morrison, John: 35, 43.
Morse, Capt. Frederick: 101.
Moss, Sidney: Arrives Oregon City 1842, 23; Hotel keeper, 58.
Mt. St. Helens: 136.
Multnomah City: 27.
Multnomah, riverboat: 166.

N

Nash, Capt. James: 169.
Navigation, Head of: At Oregon City, 29; At Milwaukie, 62, 107-8, 110-11; At Portland, 95, 108-9, 163-4; At St. Helens, 145, 149, 162.
Norton, Capt. Z. C.: 71, 163.

O

Ocean Bird, bark: 62, 79, 104.
Oregon, steamship: 84.
Oregon City: H. B. Co. post, 18; Description, 19, 23-5; Navigational handicap, 26, 29.
Oregon Territory, capital: 81.
Oregon Weekly Times: 118-9.
Oregonian, newspaper: 76-8, 79, 80.
Overton, William: 30-1.

P

Pacific Mail Steamship Co.: 83-4, 90-1, 159-68.
Panama, steamship: 84.
Perry, Francis: 138.
Pettygrove, Francis W.: Arrives Oregon City 1843, 23; Opens store, 24; Buys Portland claim, 31; Principal Portland developer, 35-44; Warehouse, 33, 35; Road to Tualatin, 36; Sells Portland interests, 43; Toast to Oregon, 45; Reminiscences, 46.
Peytona, steamship: 168-72.
Plymouth, town: 135.
Political affiliations of townsite promoters: 68, 74, 79, 127.
Polynesian, newspaper: Reports gold discovery, 48.

Portland: Description in 1846, 36; in 1847, 42-3; in 1849, 50; in 1850, 71; in 1851, 144; in 1852, 154; Couch anchors at "The Clearing" 1842, 29-30; Naming, 32; First survey, 32-3; Wharf, 35; First frame house, 35; Roads, 36; Stumps in streets, 43, 71, 144; Steam sawmill, 69-70, 151; Population, 42, 46, 126; Riverboat traffic, 155; Navigation, 95, 163; Brick pavement, 143; Steamship terminus, 163, 171.
Portland & Valley Plank Road Co.: 150-3.
Post Office Bar: 162.
Prices: In 1840s, 34, 44, 61, 115, 159; During Gold Rush, 51.

R

Railroad promotion: By Portland, 148-9; By St. Helens, 149.
Reed, Cyrus: 69.
Roads: Portland to Tualatin, 36, 146; St. Helens to Tualatin, 147.
Roberts, Capt. G. W.: 104.
Robin's Nest, early townsite: 27.
Ross Island Bar: 29, 108-9; 113-4; 161.

S

St. Helens: 102, 127, 130-7, 145, 162, 166.
St. Johns: 127, 129-30.
Sanborn, Charles: 100.
Sauvie (Sauvé), Laurent: 11.
Schnebly, D. J.: 74, 80.
Sea Gull, steamship: 85, 90.
Sequin, brig: 51, 71.
Shark, U.S.N. schooner: 37.
Skookum Chuck, riverboat: 78.
Smith, Thomas H.: 127, 138, 157, 174.
Southerner, steamship: 173.
Spectator, newspaper: 14, 26, 41, 48-9, 73, 112.
Stark, Benjamin: Cargomaster on *Toulon*, 34; Buys interest in Portland, 34; Describes Gold Rush, 52-3; Portland tract, 64, 67; Senator, 68; Visits Portland, 94.
Statesman, newspaper: 80-1.
Stephens, James: East Portland claim, 39-40.
Stephens, Thomas: 108.
Stevens, Charles: 122-3, 166.
Success, bark: 112.

Sultana, vessel: 8.
Swan Island Bar: 162, 163, 164.

T

Tappan, William H.: 127, 135-6, 155-6.
Terwilliger, James: 36-7.
Thornton, J. Q.: Describes Portland in 1847, 42; Describes St. Helens, 134.
Thurston, Samuel: 80, 111.
Torrence, William: 61.
Toulon, bark: 33, 34, 41, 45.
Trade: Oregon and Hawaii, 24; Outbound cargoes, 45, 155; Lumber, 51, 53, 61, 62; Number of vessels, 53.
Tualatin Plains (or Tualatin Valley): 106, 125, 127, 128, 130.

U

U.S. Army: Vancouver band, 100; Vancouver garrison, 135.

V

Vancouver, Capt. George: 136.
Victoria, ship: 23.

W

Wait, Aaron: Editor of *Spectator*, 48-9.

Waller, Rev. Alvin: Mission store at Oregon City, 20.
Wappatoo Island (Sauvie Island): 10.
Waterman, John O.: 73, 96, 118-9.
Waymire, John: 35.
Western Star, newspaper: Begins publication, 73-5; Politics, 74; Moves to Portland, 118-9.
Whitcomb, Lot: Biography, 57-9; Founds Milwaukie, 56; Builds schooners, 56; Ships lumber, 56, 59; Commissary - General, 58 - 9; Postmaster, 63; Builds steamboat, 96-8, 102; In politics, 119-21; Death, 123-4.
White, Bartholomew: 133.
White, Elijah: 17, 22.
Whiton, bark: 42.
Willamette, steamboat: 90, 112, 116, 159, 160-1, 162.
Williams, Posey: 138.
Williams, Richard: Captain of *Eagle*, 115.
Wilson, A. E.: Store manager, 22.
Wyeth, Nathaniel: First trip to Oregon 1832, 7; Second trip to Oregon 1834, 8-9; Establishes Fort William, 10; Abandons venture, 10-11.